BANEFUL!

95 of the World's Worst Herbs

BANEFUL!

95 of the World's Worst Herbs

Deborah J. Martin, M.H.

Copyright ©2013 Deborah J. Martin
Cover art by Kit Foster Design

All rights reserved. No part of this book may be used or reproduced by any means, graphic, electronic, or mechanical, including photocopying, recording, taping or by any information storage retrieval system without the written permission of the publisher except in the case of brief quotations embodied in critical articles and reviews.

ISBN: 978-0-9888547-2-7 (print)
ISBN: 978-0-9888547-3-4 (digital)

Published in the United States of America by The Herby Lady, LLC

The author of this book does not dispense medical advice or prescribe the use of any technique as a form of treatment for physical, emotional, or medical problems without the advice of a physician, either directly or indirectly. The intent of the author is only to offer information of a general nature. In the event you use any of the information in this book for yourself, which is your constitutional right, the author and publisher assume no responsibility for your actions.

CONTENTS

Preface	1
Acknowledgements	2
Introduction	3
Section One: The Big Eight of Antiquity	7
Aconitum spp.	10
Atropa belladonna	16
Bryonia spp.	21
Conium maculatum	25
Datura stramonium	30
Helleborus spp.	37
Hyoscyamus niger	42
Mandragora officinarum	46
Section Two: Useful, But …	53
Acorus calamus	54
Aesculus hippocastanum	59
Aloe ferox	63

Arnica montana	66
Arum maculatum	69
Baptisia tinctoria	73
Berberis vulgaris	75
Borago officinalis	77
Brassica nigra	81
Caulophyllum thalactroides	84
Chelidonium majus	87
Cinnamomum camphora	90
Citrus aurantium	93
Convallaria majalis	96
Crocus sativus	100
Cytisus scoparius	105
Digitalis purpurea	109
Fumaria officinalis	112
Gaultheria procumbens	116
Gossypium spp.	119
Gymnema sylvestre	122

Hydrastis canadensis	124
Laburnum anagyroides	127
Lobelia inflata	130
Lycopodium clavatum	134
Malus domestica	137
Mentha pulegium	141
Momordica charantia	144
Myristica fragrans	146
Phaseolus lunatus	149
Phytolacca spp.	153
Podophyllum peltatum	157
Pulsaltilla vulgaris	159
Rhamnus cathartica	162
Sanguinaria canadensis	166
Sassafras officinale	169
Simmondsia chinensis	173
Solanum tuberosum	175
Viscum album	179

Section Three: In the Garden 183

Alkanna tinctoria 184

Anagallis arvensis 187

Aquilegia vulgaris 191

Asclepias tuberosa 194

Brugmansia suaveolens 197

Buxus sempervirens 201

Chrysanthemum vulgare 204

Cyclamen persicum 207

Daphne spp. 210

Delphinium spp. 214

Dictamnus albus 217

Hedera helix 220

Ilex aquifolium 223

Kalanchoe lanceolata 226

Narcissum spp. 229

Prunus laurocerasus 232

Rheum raponticum 235

Rhododendron spp.	239
Ruta graveolens	243
Thuja occidentalis	247
Section Four: Let's Get High	251
Agave tequilana	252
Amanita muscaria	256
Areca catechu	260
Artemisia absinthium	264
Cannabis sativa	270
Cola spp.	275
Convulvulus spp.	279
Lactuca virosa	284
Papaver somniferum	288
Pausinystalia yohimbe	293
Turnera diffusa	297
Section Five: Really Awful	301
Abrus precatorius	302
Cerbera odollam	305

Cicuta spp.	309
Colchicum autumnale	313
Diffenbachia seguine	316
Euonymus europaeus	319
Gelsemium spp.	323
Juniperus sabina	326
Kalmia latifolia	329
Larrea tridentata	332
Melia azedarach	335
Nerium oleander	338
Physostigma venenosum	342
Rhus toxicodendron	344
Ricinus communis	347
Strychnos nux-vomica	350
Taxus baccata	353
Cheat Sheet (common to Latin)	357
Bibliography	362
Illustrations	367

PREFACE

Let's get the legalities out of the way, shall we? I'll even put it in big, bold letters so it nobody over looks it.

The information presented in this book is for informational and educational purposes only. The plants mentioned herein can cause harm or even death. *In no way* **do I suggest you ingest, inhale, in-anything any of the plants mentioned in this book. Nor do I suggest you use them on any human or other animal, with or without their knowledge. Should you choose to do so, any and all consequences of your actions are yours and yours alone. I take no responsibility for the actions of anyone who does not heed this or any other warning in this book.**

Got it? Good.

ACKNOWLEDGEMENTS

As with all my herb books, I can't take all the credit. So many have come before me over the centuries, sharing their knowledge in print and now online. All I did was pull it all together.

My friends on TW: you gave me a starting place and kept nudging me toward the finish line. For that I will always be grateful. On a *very* personal note: Aloe, *don't eat this book!*

Editor extraordinaire and crazy herb lady in her own right, Laura Perry, not only corrected the grammatical faux pas but challenged some of the entries. By doing so, she made it a *much* better book.

Finally, my husband Pete. He may not know a damned thing about herbs or witchcraft but he loves me. (I continually question his sanity in that regard.) His love and support is what keeps me going.

INTRODUCTION

Baneful *adj. Webster's* defines it as poisonous, pernicious, destructive, deadly. Princeton University's *Wordnetweb* say it means exceedingly harmful. *Oxford English Dictionary* says it's an archaic word, meaning poisonous. I like their current definition of the noun, bane, "cause of great distress or annoyance". Perhaps a better definition of baneful would be "causing great distress or annoyance".

Although most people think "poisonous", you'll find the word used by agrarian types when referring to plants that are invasive and/or pernicious – any unwanted plant that threatens to take over or destroy a cash crop. (For readers in the southern United States, think Kudzu.)

If you've done any research into herbs, you know that virtually *any* plant can cause distress if used improperly, in too large quantities or by someone who has an allergy to that plant. Using my better definition, any of the Mints could be baneful to a couple trying to conceive. (Mint can lower sperm count.)

In the context of this book, I am using the word "baneful" in its broadest sense: plants that can range from relatively safe when used properly (Common Ivy) to deadly (Castor). As Paracelsus wrote in the sixteenth century, "In all things there is a poison, and there is nothing without a poison. It depends only upon the dose whether a poison is poison or not." They all have uses: many in a medicinal sense when administered by someone with proper knowledge; many for astral travel, hedge riding, Otherworld experiences (whatever you want to call it); and many for other magical purposes.

There are well over a thousand poisonous plants on this Earth. This book is not intended to be a comprehensive reference to them all. Instead, I chose those I thought were the most interesting: they may be found in everyday gardens; they may have stories about them; or the historical applications are … curious.

As is my custom, I have listed all plants by their Latin binomial with a cheat sheet at the back. Due to the insane number of common names for many plants, this method is much less confusing and makes for easier reference. Under each plant, you will find a toxicity level: Level I being the worst toxicity known to man; down to Level III, harmful in some instances.

If you choose to work with baneful plants, ensure you not only have identified the plant correctly but that you know *which* part of the plant is poisonous and possibly *when* it's bad for you. As a prime example, the majority of us eat potatoes on a regular basis. Ripe potatoes are good and good for you. However, this plant is a member of the Nightshade (*Solanum*) family. Its leaves and the unripe tuber *are* poisonous.

Also understand that it's not necessarily ingestion of the plant that can harm you. Many are baneful by absorption through the skin, smoking, or simply inhaling the fumes or plant particles, such as Yew sawdust. Take proper precautions such as using gloves or wearing a mask when working with baneful plants.

Lastly, *every plant (or one of its parts) listed in this book is a poison in the broadest sense of the word.* Take heed.

Now, on to one of my favorite subjects: Baneful Herbs.

SECTION ONE

The Big Eight of Antiquity

Long before science was able to separate out the different compounds in plants to safely decide what was poisonous and what wasn't, Man knew certain plants could cause death. People probably learned this through trial and error – someone either noticed a four-legged animal eat a plant and die, or someone foolishly ate a plant and keeled over.

Then there's Mithridates VI, King of Pontus (134 – 63 BCE), who was considered an expert toxicologist in his time. As poisoning was a very effective assassination tool back then, he determined to fortify himself against any and all poisons. He experimented with herbs and dosages to the detriment of many a slave, trying to find the perfect dose of each herb – one that was not lethal but would inure his body to the toxins. Once he determined the recipe, he is reported to have taken a little every day to build up his immunity. It's said the antidote he finally perfected was so good that when he tried to commit suicide by poison, he couldn't find one that had any effect. Reports differ but whether suicide or murder, he ended up dying by the sword. There are many stories of his recipe (some say as many as sixty-five ingredients), alterations thereto, and its use throughout the ages. Today, the word "mithridate" is a generally-accepted term for any all-purpose antidote.

According to Richard Evan Schultes, the "Big Four" poisons of the Middle Ages were Thorn Apple, Mandrake, Henbane and Belladonna. (*Datura spp., Mandragora officinarum, Hyoscamus niger* and *Atropa belladonna*). To that, I am adding *Aconitum spp., Bryonia spp., Conium maculatum* and *Helleborus spp.* One can't talk about poisons of Antiquity without including those, as well.

Bear in mind that under the right conditions, any and all of these plants were and are still used for beneficial purposes. In the 15th century, doctors made what was known as the "Sleeping Apple". According to Giambattista della Porta (*Natural Magic*, 1558) it was "made of Opium, Mandrake, juice of Hemlock, the seeds of Henbane, and adding a little musk to gain an easier reception from the smeller; these being made up into a ball, as big as a man's hand can hold, and often smelt to, gently close the eyes, and bind them with a deep sleep". Perhaps this was the inspiration for the apple we all know from the Grimms' Fairy Tale about SnowDrop (Snow White for you Disney fans).

Aconitum napellus
Monkshood, Aconite, Wolfsbane, Leopard's Bane, Friar's Cap, Mousebane

Description: There are more than 300 Species of *Aconitum* with various levels of toxicity and medicinal actions. *A. napellus* is considered the "official" Aconite. A perennial native to Europe, it is now cultivated in the Americas. It grows up to three feet high, with a very erect stem; palmate, dark green, glossy leaves; and hood-like, blue/purple flowers. It generally flowers during the height of summer. The root is often mistaken for horseradish.

Cultivation: Aconite prefers a slightly damp, loamy soil and flourishes best in full shade. Sow seeds after the danger of frost has passed, thinning to one foot apart after several leaves have appeared. It generally takes two to three years to flower. Propagate by root division in the autumn, after the stem has died back. Although the plant lasts more than one year, the main root does not. It develops "daughter roots" which sprout the next year, thus continuing the life of the plant. It is these "daughter roots" which should be separated for propagation.

Parts Used: Whole plant.

Poison: Entire plant, especially the root. Toxicity Level I.

Side Effects: Ingestion of Aconite paralyzes nerves, lowers blood pressure, and stops the heart. Skin contact can cause numbness, nerve tingling and cardiac symptoms. 10-15 grams of the dried root is lethal to humans.

Medicinal Uses: Aconite was first used as a *medicine* by Baron Störck of Vienna: he published his results in 1762. From the *US Dispensatory of 1834*: "In moderate doses it excites the circulation, increases the perspiratory and urinary discharge, and exercises considerable influence over the nervous system. […] Its constitutional effects are also experienced when it is applied to the surface of a wound. […] Its highest reputation has perhaps been as a remedy in obstinate rheumatism." In current medicine, it is used externally as an anodyne for neuralgia, lumbago and rheumatism. Although it's recognized as poisonous, the

Blackfeet use a preparation of the root for fevers, acute respiratory infection and throat infections. Also used in some indigenous cultures as a psychoactive drug. The root and seeds are also powdered, mixed with oil and rubbed on the scalp to kill lice and cure dandruff.

Magical Uses: Well known since ancient times as an ingredient in the witch's flying ointment. Some witches chewed the leaves for the anesthetic and hallucinogenic effect. (Only witches could do this without suffering any ill effects.) Also used for Banishing, Courage, Curing and Protection. Supposedly, carrying a root on one's person or tying a bag containing a root around the neck of livestock would ward off all vermin.

Interesting Tidbits: According to Pliny, Aconae, a town on the Black Sea, was held in ill repute because of all the Aconite growing nearby. This, in theory, is where the Genus got its name.

It's well-known as an arrow poison. It probably got one of its common names, Wolfsbane, due to the fact that the Ancient Greeks used it on the tips of their spears when hunting wolves. The Aleut also use it as a fish and whale poison, and it's still used today in India by poachers hunting elephants for their ivory.

Greek mythology says that Aconite grew from the spit of Cerberus (the three-headed dog who guarded the way into the Underworld). Wherever he drooled, there grew an Aconite plant. It's also supposedly the "poison cup" Medea prepared for Theseus, trying to preserve her own son's inheritance. (This mythical Aconite probably isn't *Aconitum napellus* – it's not native to Greece.) Pliny speaks of "Old Wife's-hood" (probably *A. anthora*) as the fastest-working poison and at the time it was referred to as "woman's murder". It was known that death would occur the same day if applied to a woman's genitals.

To hide it, the Greeks sold the juice in hollowed-out horns. It needed hiding: in 1st century Greece, poisoning by Aconite was a capital offense due to the lack of a known antidote. However, the government wasn't totally against its use: on the island of Ceos, it was the law that elderly people no longer able to earn a living take Aconite to spare their family the cost of their upkeep.

Aconite as a murder weapon made its way to Rome. It was not only used by individuals with a grudge but by professional poisoners as well. Murder by Aconite was so popular that the emperor Trajan banned the cultivation of the plant in Roman gardens in 117 CE. As late as the 16th century in both Prague and Italy, it was used on criminals as a way to "refine" execution techniques.

Scholars debate the subject, but it's possible that Aconite is what Romeo drank. From *Romeo and Juliet*, Act V, Scene I: "Let me have a dram of poison, such soon-speeding gear; As will disperse itself through all veins; That the life-weary taker may fall dead; And that the trunk may be discharged of breath; as violently as hasty powder fired."

At one time, horse dealers used to feed Aconite to their animals before taking them to market. Its strong intoxicating effect made them appear more lively and, hopefully, more appealing to purchasers.

Notes:

Atropa belladonna

Atropa belladonna
Belladonna, Deadly Nightshade, Dwale, Banewort, Devil's Cherry

Description: A perennial widely distributed throughout Central and Southern Europe and seen in the wild on occasion in the United States. The thick root sends up a stout stem that usually divides into three branches that can grow up to five feet high. The dull green leaves grow in pairs – one small, one large. The flowers are dark purple and bell-shaped, appearing in June or July. The berry (about the size of a cherry and shiny black) generally ripens in September. The stems will lose their leaves in the fall but it is indeed a perennial.

Cultivation: Sow seeds in very moist, slightly chalky soil after the danger of frost has passed. Thin to two to three feet apart when the plants are 1½ inches tall. Belladonna prefers full shade. Propagation from cuttings should occur in late spring. Belladonna, being a member of the Nightshade family, is subject to the same pests as tomatoes and potatoes.

Parts Used: Medicinally, the leaves. Magically, the whole plant.

Poison: The entire plant. Toxicity Level I. (The berries are very sweet and are a dangerous temptation for children.)

Side Effects: Ingestion causes rapid heartbeat, confusion, hallucinations and seizures with increasing paralysis, damage to the respiratory system, coma and death. Contact dermatitis is possible simply by touching any part of the plant.

Medicinal Uses: In the Middle Ages, the juice of Belladonna was mixed with the juice of henna, warmed, and then dropped into the ear to cure an earache; the leaves were soaked in vinegar and applied to the forehead to ease headaches. Later, the leaves were used externally for tumors, cancers and other ulcers, and Belladonna preparations were used for "nervous diseases" such as whooping cough and neuralgia. Even today, in low doses, a tincture of the leaves is used for a depressant and sedative effect. A chemical extract of the herb, Atropine, is still used by ophthalmologists to dilate eyes but only in cases where they want the effects of the drug to degrade slowly, generally 7-14 days.

Magical Uses: It's a popular herb as an aid in astral projection or to produce visions. Some cultures use it in rituals for Banishing, Protection, Purification and Transitions.

Interesting Tidbits: Many people think that the name "Belladonna" (pretty lady) arises from the habit of Italian women of the Middle Ages and Renaissance dropping either the juice or a tincture of the berries into their eyes to dilate their pupils, thus making them alluring. (It would *sting*. The things ladies do to attract a man!) Other legends say it was named Belladonna because at times it takes the form of a lovely enchantress, whom it is dangerous to look upon. And yet a third possible origin is thought to be from the ritual of priests who drank an infusion of Belladonna prior to worshipping and invoking the name of Bellona, the goddess of war. The Genus name, Atropa, is from the Greek Fate Atropos, who brought death at the time and manner of her choosing.

The common name, Dwale, is from the Anglo-Saxon word meaning stupefying drink or perhaps from the Scandinavian "Dvale" – stupor.

Stories tell us this plant is sacred to Hecate and should be picked on May Eve. Yet another legend says this plant belongs to the devil, who trims and tends it in his leisure. The only way to harvest the plant for yourself while he's diverted from his care is on Walpurgis, when he's preparing for the witches' Sabbath that night.

The juice was once used as a spear poison for hunting. Pliny noted that spears tipped with Belladonna juice retained their toxicity for thirty years.

Marc Antony's soldiers ate Belladonna berries. Although the berries are the *least* poisonous part of the plant, these soldiers went insane for awhile and many of them lost their memory.

The juice was used during the Burning Times to deaden pain … not only from torture or burning but also from childbirth.

Notes

Bryonia spp.

White Bryony (*Bryonia alba*), Red Bryony (*Bryonia dioica*), English Mandrake, Devil's Turnip, Wild Vine, Wild Hops

Description: There are 12 Eurasian and North African Species; white and red are cultivated in the United States. All carry the same toxic qualities; all are very similar looking plants. Bryony is a perennial vine that climbs via tendrils arising from the side of the leaf stalks. The vines die back after the fruit has ripened. The leaves have a curved stalk with five lobes. Small, greenish flowers bloom in May; stamens and pistils are never found together in the same flower. The berries are about the size of a pea and when ripe, are either black (*B. alba*) or pale red (*B. dioica*).

Cultivation: After the danger of frost has passed, sow seeds in almost any soil, in a spot where the plant will get full sun. Since this is a climber, it's recommended you provide a trellis if there isn't a natural one nearby.

Parts Used: The root.

Poison: The entire plant, especially the fruit and bark. Toxicity Level I.

Side Effects: Ingestion causes vomiting, drastic and bloody diarrhea, and death from respiratory arrest. 6-8 berries are enough to cause vomiting in adults. The entire plant is a skin irritant.

Medicinal Uses: No longer used in a medicinal sense, except in homeopathy for various disorders where the patient is a "grumpy bear". Although it has possible anti-tumor activity, it is considered too poisonous to use by researchers. It was used up until Renaissance times as a violent purgative and a decoction of the root in wine was drunk once a week at bedtime to "expel a dead child" – as an abortifacient. In the 14th century, it was used as an antidote to leprosy.

In 14th century France, it was known as "Herb of Beaten Wives" – an ointment of Bryony was used to reduce bruising.

Magical Uses: There is very little published on this subject. Augustus Caesar wore a wreath of Bryony to protect himself from lightning. Polish mythology says that if White Bryony was found on one's property, the plant should be fenced it to protect it; the leaves resemble a child and digging it up would destroy the family's happiness. Some consider the red berries of *B. dioica* to be a powerful ingredient in love spells.

Interesting Tidbits: Because Mandrake was difficult (and expensive) to obtain in the British Isles, White Bryony root, plentiful in England, was used as a substitute – it is occasionally anthropomorphic in shape. However, hucksters preyed on those wanting a Mandrake root for love or fertility spells: they would either trim the Bryony root to make it look like a Mandrake or carefully fix a mold over a young Bryony root. Said root would then grow into the shape of the mold which was, naturally, of that of a man or woman.

Notes:

Conium maculatum

Conium maculatum
(Poison) Hemlock, Poison Parsley, Herb Bennet

Description: A biennial plant found throughout Europe and North America, usually alongside roads or in waste area. It is a tall, graceful plant, growing from two to eight feet high. The smooth, erect stem is bright green but mottled with red. The leaves resemble Parsley or Queen Anne's Lace, for which it is often and fatally mistaken. (If in doubt, crush the plant. It gives off a very disagreeable odor.) The flowers, which appear from June to August, are white and the fruit, which can be mistaken for Anise seeds, are grayish brown.

Cultivation: Hemlock will grow just about anywhere in any conditions. It does prefer a sunny location and slightly moist soil.

Parts Used: The root.

Poison: The entire plant. Toxicity Level I.

Effects: The first sensations are a burning feeling in the mouth and throat, leading to drowsiness, trembling, nausea, vomiting and diarrhea. Eventual symptoms include mental disturbance and paralysis of motor nerve endings, starting at the extremities and ending with respiratory failure and death.

Medicinal Uses: Still used in minute doses as a sedative and antispasmodic. In the Middle Ages, Hemlock was used in sleeping draughts; in preparations to kill head lice; and with Henbane, as a poultice for sore knees. As late as 1867, Hemlock was considered a palliative treatment for cancerous complaints, cirrhosis of the liver and painful skin diseases. They even thought a proper dose suitable treatment for hyperactive children.

Magical Uses: Hemlock is associated with toads in German folklore. The toads are thought to absorb the poison of Hemlock and thus become poisonous themselves. It was used in love spells in Antiquity: supposedly a poultice of Hemlock was used to "abate" love. Although they know it's poisonous, the women of the Klallan tribe rub the root on their body to attract a man.

Interesting Tidbits: No discussion of Poison Hemlock would be complete without mentioning Socrates, who was sentenced to death in Athens for "corrupting the youth and impiety". Plato described his death in his *Phaedo*, saying that Socrates was lucid until the end. Theophrastus speculates that Socrates drank a compound of Hemlock and Opium but due to the soporific nature of Opium, the stories would then conflict.

Two professional poisoners of Rome, Apollodorus and Canidia used Hemlock preserved in honey.

In Old English, Hemlock is called "Wodewhistel". The stems, which are hollow, were used as pea shooters. (The poisonous qualities diminish greatly when the plant has dried.) The stem was also harvested in autumn and used as reeds when weaving worsted threads.

According to English legend, the red/purple streaks on the stem represent the brand put on Cain's brow after he murdered Abel.

It is still known in Scotland as "deid man's oatmeal".

Notes:

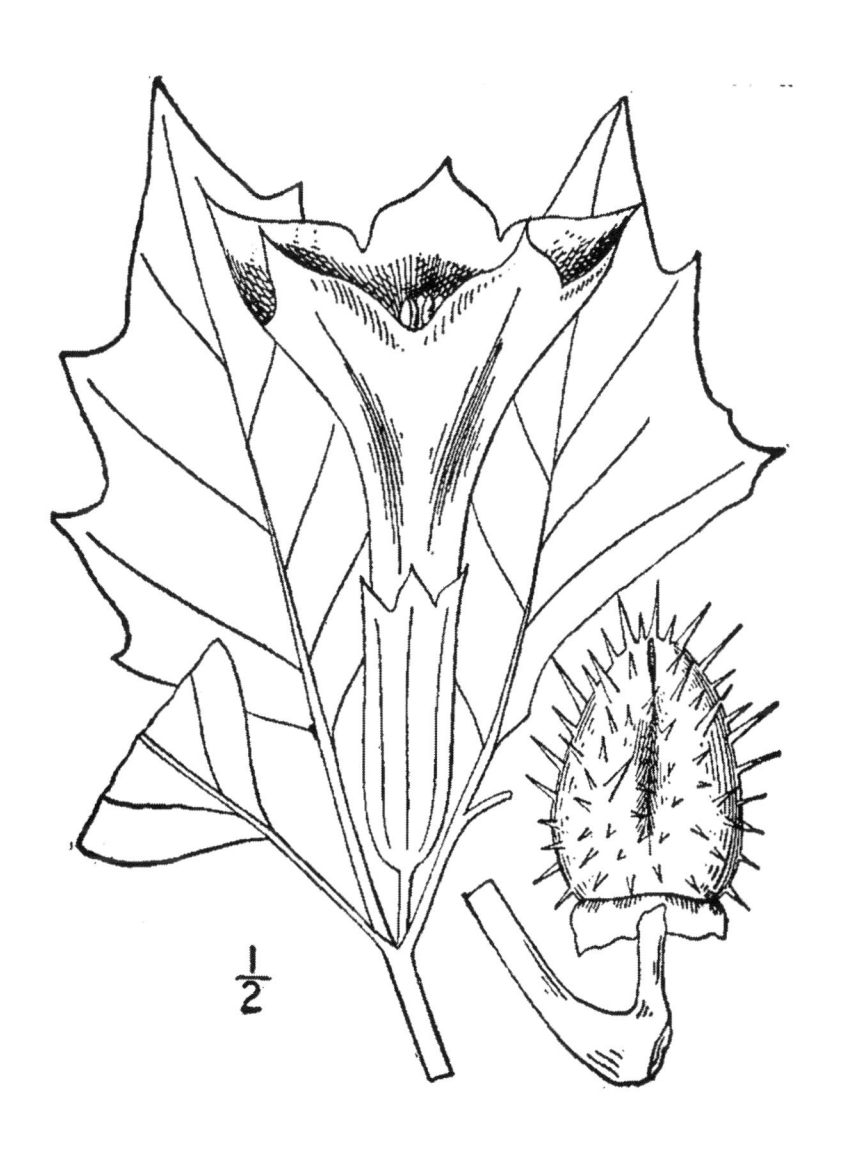

Datura stramonium

Datura spp.

Datura, Jimsonweed, Thornapple, Devil's Weed, Angel's Trumpet

Description: There are nine Species in this Genus, all of similar toxic properties. *D. stramonium* is common in the New World (the Americas) and *D. metel* was the most important Species in the Old World for medicinal and hallucinogenic uses. *D. stramonium* is a large, bushy annual, growing three to five feet high and spreading out almost as broad. The leaves are broad, dark green on top and a lighter green below. The showy flowers are white and bloom nearly all summer. The fruit is oval, slightly prickly, and contains many seeds.

Cultivation: All Species of Datura will grow easily in an open, sunny location. Although it will grow in most any soil, a rich loam will yield better results. Sow after the danger of frost has passed, about three feet apart and barely covered. One needn't worry about ensuring the seeds are fresh: tests have shown that Datura seeds stored for 39 years will still yield a 90% germination rate.

Parts Used: The whole plant.

Poison: The entire plant. Toxicity Level I.

Side Effects: High doses produce powerful hallucinations, euphoria, confusion, convulsions, respiratory failure and death.

Medicinal Uses: Peruvian physicians used the seeds of Datura as an anesthetic during trepanning operations; cultures in the southwestern United States and Mexico also employed it as an anesthetic and analgesic to relieve pain during operations. It is still used as an analgesic, as an ingredient in cough syrup and is smoked to treat asthma. Native Americans used the leaves as a poultice for boils and wounds and in an ointment as an analgesic while setting broken bones. In World War II, Datura was a cash crop for the English – the leaves were used in powders and cigarettes used to treat asthma.

During the Sanskrit period, *D. metel* was used in India to treat mental disorders, fevers, tumors, breast inflammation, skin disorders and diarrhea.

Although it was already known as a powerful narcotic, Störck used *D. stramonium* internally to treat cases of mania and epilepsy, and externally in an ointment for ulcers, inflamed tumors, mastalgia and hemorrhoids. It was said that the effects of an "appropriate dose" would "pass off in five or six hours, or in a shorter period, and no inconvenience is subsequently experienced".

A 1920's edition of the American Medical Journal lists *D. stramonium* as a remedy for hydrophobia (rabies).

Magical Uses: Used by shamans in many indigenous cultures to transcend reality. Datura is an ingredient in many flying ointments. In the Middle Ages and beyond, it was considered to aid the incantations of witches. During the Burning Times, it was considered unlucky to have it growing in one's garden. (If you were growing it, you, of course, were a witch.) It is also used to counteract spells and hexes.

Several cultures indigenous to the United States have used Datura during rites of passage such as male initiation rituals and ceremonies to honor a recently deceased member of the tribe.

The Paiute chew the seeds for good luck when gambling. A Zuni who was the victim of a robbery would chew the root to find the thief.

Interesting Tidbits: Due to the narcotic nature of Datura, many stories abound of its use. It was possibly the medieval version of a date rape drug – it was used as an aid in seduction where women were on the receiving end.

It was used by priestesses in ancient Greece for divinatory purposes.

Datura has long been associated with the worship of Shiva, who represents the creative and destructive aspects of the universe.

Legend has it that robbers (and Indian prostitutes) would spike the drink of their intended victim with powdered seeds. The victim would be witless and unable to defend themselves against the robbery. It didn't always work: in the 1800's Bassawar Singh mixed Datura seeds in a curry for some fellow travelers in India. Apparently they didn't like his cooking enough to eat a lot, as they recovered and reported him to the British police. He tried to be clever and ate some of his own curry. He died.

The common name for *D. stramonium*, Jimsonweed, is probably a corruption of "Jamestown Weed". When Jamestown was colonized in 1607, the colonists found a beautiful weed growing plentifully at the site. They made the fatal mistake of trying to add it to their diet. When the British attacked several decades later, the colonists remembered the experience and slipped Datura into the British soldiers' food. The soldiers went crazy for eleven days, allowing the colonists to temporarily gain the upper hand.

Abraham Lincoln's mother, Nancy Hanks, was apparently the victim of Datura poisoning: she drank milk from a cow that had grazed on the plant, developed "milk sickness" and wasted away. This event, in theory, is why the President abstained from drinking alcohol for the rest of his life.

One research source suggested that Datura can be used to clean up soil pollution. Terence McKenna suggests, "The shrub *Datura stramonium* can act like a toxin sponge, leaching heavy-metal elements from polluted soils. The toxins are concentrated in its tissue, which can then be removed".

Notes:

Helleborus viridis

Helleborus spp.
Hellebore

Description: There are twenty-one Species in this Genus, all with similar toxic properties. *H. niger* (Black Hellebore) is native to Central and Southern Europe. *H. viridis* (Green Hellebore) is native to both Europe and North America. All Species carry the same level of toxicity. It's a perennial herb that typically grows by rhizomes that put out a low-growing stalk – the flower stalks rise directly from the root and take several years to flower. The leaves are deeply-lobed and the flowers are generally white. Black Hellebore blooms in midwinter, earning it the common name of Christmas Rose.

Cultivation: All Species of Hellebore will grow easily in any garden soil but some prefer a slightly rich soil. They only like moist soil (do not allow the roots to be oversaturated) and partial sun; a location as an understory to trees or shrubbery is preferable. Propagation is generally by seed or root division.

Parts Used: The root.

Poison: The entire plant but especially the aerial portion. Toxicity Level I.

Side Effects: High doses produce rapid death due to heart failure. Symptoms may include nausea, dilated pupils, gastric distress, and respiratory and cardiac irregularities. Contact with mucous membranes produces bleeding and blisters; the sap can cause skin irritation.

Medicinal Uses: It is no longer used medicinally. In earlier times it was used as a sneezing powder; to treat constipation, nausea and intestinal worms; and as an abortifacient. In the Middle Ages, a pea-sized dose (taken at Midsummer only) "drives out all old, serious and untreatable ailments".

Paracelsus and the ancient Greeks believed that the plant had a rejuvenating effect: white Hellebore for people under the age of 50; black Hellebore for those over the mid-century mark. It was "gathered when the moon was in one of the conservation phases, dried in an east wind, mixed with its own weight of sugar and a pinch was taken each morning and evening" (Mrs. C.F. Leyel, citing Paracelsus in *Magic of Herbs*, 1926).

Magical Uses: Hellebore is an ingredient in flying ointments and also used as an aid to astral projection. The root of Black Hellebore, powdered and scattered on the ground grants invisibility.

The music emanating from a harp made of hellebore wood will cure sciatica and also rouse one from sleep.

Hellebore in an ingredient in spells for banishing, cursing and endings.

Interesting Tidbits: Horticulturists collecting the seeds of *H. foetidus* in 2001 had their fingerprints burned off for several weeks.

In the 15th and 16th centuries, *H. niger* was grafted onto grape vines. The toxin will eventually enter the grapes and the wine made from these was used to cause abortions.

Odysseus tipped his arrows with Hellebore in Homer's *Odyssey*.

Ancient Gaulish hunters would tip their spears with Black Hellebore. Because the flesh of the prey animal would then also be poisoned, there was a race to cut the infected meat away from the arrow wound. The Gauls knew of at least two antidotes to Hellebore poisoning: there was always the worry of a self-inflicted wound when applying the paste to the spear tips.

Although scholars aren't certain, it is speculated that Alexander the Great died after taking a medication including Hellebore.

Notes:

Hyocyamus niger

Hyoscyamus niger
Henbane, Hog's Bean, Stinking Roger

Description: Fifteen Species make up the Genus *Hyoscyamus*, all similar. The plant is either annual or biennial, and you can get different forms from the same crop of seeds. It grows up to two feet tall with grayish-green hairy leaves spreading from a crown. The annual will flower later than the biennial form. The petals of the flower are white to grayish with purple veins.

Cultivation: Henbane grows with a mind of its own: sometimes seeds won't germinate at all; sometimes they'll germinate after a year or two. It will grow in most any soil but moderately-rich, well-drained soil in a sunny location is best. Sow as soon as the ground is warm, thinning seedlings to two feet apart. It is a member of the Solanaceae family and subject to the same pest issues as tomatoes and the other cousins.

Parts Used: The aerial portion of the plant.

Poison: The entire plant. Toxicity Level I. Neither drying nor boiling the herb reduces the toxicity.

Side Effects: It's been well-known since Antiquity as a mind-altering drug. Even the aroma arising from the leaves can cause giddiness and stupor. High doses produce hallucinations, dilated pupils and a rapid pulse. Death results from respiratory arrest. As few as 15 seeds can cause death in children.

Medicinal Uses: No longer used as a medicinal herb; chemical extracts are used in ophthalmology and to treat gastrointestinal spasms. Until the invention of ether and chloroform in the 19th century, Henbane was used as an anesthetic and as a sedative but was considered inferior to opium in that regard. It does, however, have one advantage over opium: it does not produce constipation. The leaves were smoked to relieve asthma; it was administered to alleviate the pain of a toothache and as a treatment for nervous disorders and insomnia.

In the 16th century, Henbane leaves were cast upon coals and the rising smoke was directed through a paper tunnel to cure "chopped" (chapped) lips. The same method was used to drive out tooth worms (believed to cause tooth decay).

Culpeper would boil the leaves in wine and use them to treat swellings of a man's testicles or a woman's breast. He also used a decoction of either the herb or seeds to kill lice.

Magical Uses: An ingredient in flying ointments. Also used to call up "evil entities"; to induce clairvoyance; in countermagic spells; and to attract the love of a woman.

Albertus Magnus (died circa 1280 CE) wrote, "Those who occupy themselves with magic, report that a figure, on whom one wishes to cast a spell, must be sketched with the juice of this herb".

Henbane was used in medieval German rituals to bring rain.

Interesting Tidbits: In German, Henbane is called Hexenkraut, "witches' herb".

It is believed that Henbane is strongest at the Summer Solstice. Therefore, it should be gathered at the feast-day of

John the Baptist (June 24th). In England, an old belief said that the herb was most potent when gathered by a virgin standing only on her right foot, using her pinkie to pull the plant from the ground.

In Gaul, Henbane was gathered by loosening the soil around the plant with a dagger; the stem was attached to the leg of a trained bird who then uprooted the plant when it flew up.

The Dead in Hades were crowned with leaves of Henbane as they wandered by the river Styx.

Henbane was added to beer in the Middle Ages to enhance the beverage's intoxicating effects.

It was a common means of suicide and murder in antiquity and medieval times, as well as being used to relieve the suffering of those sentenced to torture and/or death.

Henbane leaves will crackle loudly when burned, as if they contain a nitrate.

Notes:

Mandragora officinarum
Mandrake, Mandragora, Satan's Apple, Devil's Apple

Description: A perennial plant that is native to Southern Europe. It is almost stem-less with large, dark green, pointed leaves. A solitary white or cream flower forms in early summer. (Some plants may be non-flowering.) Berries are dark yellow or orange-red and lie on the ground. The large, brown root may grow 3-4 feet deep, occasionally divides or branches and is said to have an anthropomorphic appearance.

Cultivation: May be propagated by seed. Plant in light soil in the fall for emersion in the spring. Mandrake prefers moist soil and warm conditions. If necessary, you may transplant to their final home in August. Be sure to cover for winter if you live in a harsh climate.

Parts Used: All.

Poison: All parts of the plant. Toxicity Level: leaves and fruit II; root I.

Side Effects: A low dose has depressant and sedative effects. Higher doses produce hallucinations, euphoria, confusion, and nausea. Death occurs from central nervous system paralysis.

Medicinal Uses: Of old, a small piece of root was used to induce sleep, especially for surgery; to treat eye diseases; and as an abortifacient. It is cited as an anesthetic in many medicinal manuscripts dating from the Assyrians (9th century BCE) through the Middle Ages and Renaissance, all the way to Culpeper and Gerard in the 17th century. The Ebers Papyrus (c. 1500 BCE) includes Mandrake in a recipe for intestinal worms. Another old recipe combines the pulped root with brandy for chronic rheumatism.

In the Middle Ages, the juice of the root was smeared on the face to cure insomnia and headaches. It was also used for earaches, "foot disease", muscle soreness and to cure madness, which they called "devil sickness".

The early 1900's saw the leaves of Mandrake used in poultices for skin ulcers and in other preparations, such as ointments. They are said to have a cooling property.

Mandrake is today used homeopathically and is indicated for hay fever, colic, asthma and coughs.

Magical Uses: Mandrake is an ingredient in the witch's flying ointment. It is also one of the earliest known aphrodisiacs, used by both the ancient Egyptians and Arabs. It is the Arabs who gave Mandrake fruit one of its other common names, Devil's Apple, due to its ability to produce sensual and evocative dreams.

Perhaps due to Leah's use of mandrake to conceive (Genesis 30:14-16) it was long thought to make a woman fertile. However, the same use goes back to the Babylonians, whose women carried a root as a charm against sterility. Even as late as the 1920's, women in England, Syria and Turkey still carried a piece of the root with them for that reason and in Greece, it was thought of as a love charm for either sex.

Other Biblical references involve its use in demon-expelling rings. It was specifically associated with Solomon.

The Ancient Greeks and Romans made amulets of Mandrake against bewitchment. As well, the Romans thought it would cure demonic possession. The Greeks used it in love potions.

Few herbs carry as much magical legend as Mandrake root. Due to it looking like one gender or the other (to those with strong imaginations), people in the Middle Ages and Renaissance period kept "manikins" as good luck charms. These manikins were treated with great care: after pulling the root up during the night, it was given a bath, wrapped in red and white silk and placed in a special box. It was bathed again every Friday and given a fresh wrapping at each new moon. A German tradition stated that if you placed a gold piece in the box with your manikin, you would find it doubled by morning. The manikin brought the gold into the house via the chimney.

Yet others thought the roots were either elves or dwarves. They placed their roots in dishes and fed them milk and rusks (hard, dry biscuits). Keeping the root happy meant wealth; not doing so would bring death.

In other countries of northern Europe, childless couples were said to be blessed with children thanks to a manikin.

The Apuleian traditions hold that if a Mandrake is kept in the center of the house, it will ward off harm.

Many indigenous tribes use Mandrake for banishing, controlling, courage, cursing, protection and purification.

Flavius Josephus (1st century CE) was the first to postulate the use of dogs when harvesting a Mandrake root. Specifically, one should dig around the root in a circle; tie a string from the plant to a dog's tail; and entice the dog to run away from the plant at great speed (usually with a thrown piece of meat). The dog will die as an offering to the plant.

Others compounded this superstition by saying the root should only be harvested at night; others say it is most powerful if you are able to gather it at a crossroads or from underneath a gallows. Somehow, the medieval people got the idea that to root screamed as it was pulled and hearing this scream was, if not lethal, at least enough to drive you insane. A Spanish writer in the 13th century CE claimed it wasn't the root that screamed but the devil who had lost his home and took possession of the digger.

Interesting Tidbits: The Ancients usually sliced and sun-dried the roots, then crushed or boiled them and preserved them in wine. One of Hannibal's generals, Marhabel, left such tainted wine in an enemy's camp in Africa (c. 396 BCE) as a "gift". The soldiers who drank the wine lost consciousness and were slaughtered by this general's army.

Shakespeare knew well the soporific and deadly effects of Mandrake. Cleopatra says (Antony and Cleopatra, Act I, Scene 5), "Give me to drink Mandragora [...] That I might sleep out this great gap of time, My Antony is away."

Mandrake is part of the emblem of the Association of Anesthetists of Great Britain and Ireland, due to its early role in anesthesia.

Notes:

SECTION TWO

Useful, But ...

There are many plants in use today that still need to be treated with extreme care. Yes, some are *very* useful: we eat potatoes and make clothing and other items from cotton. The gel from an Aloe leaf soothes a burn. However, each of these "useful" plants has a dangerous side to it which should engender some caution.

That said, you'll find these plants all around you. Just keep in mind what you're working with, okay?

Acorus calamus
Sweet Flag, Sweet Sedge, Gladden

Description: A perennial plant that can be found almost anywhere in the northern hemisphere, near the margins of lakes, ponds, streams and any marshy area. The root grows horizontally up to 5 feet long and produces no stalk but sword-shaped leaves with a pink base from 2 to 6 feet high. The flower stalk grows from the axil of the outer leaves, looking very much like a cattail with many minute, greenish-yellow flowers. (It never flowers unless it is growing directly in water.) If the proper insects are around for pollination, it will produce a very juicy berry. The entire plant is very sweet-smelling.

Cultivation: It is most easily cultivated from root division. Divide in early spring or at the beginning of fall and plant one foot apart in damp, muddy spots.

Parts Used: Root, rhizome.

Poison: The root. Toxicity Level: II

Side Effects: A small piece of the root is a stimulant; a larger piece will produce hallucinations. It supposedly tastes like ginger when dried and will numb the tongue.

Medicinal Uses: Calamus has been used for centuries in both Traditional Chinese Medicine and Ayurveda as a remedy for bronchitis, asthma and fevers. In China it is ingested to relieve constipation. Because of the numbing effect, it is used to treat toothache until one can get to a dentist. A fluid extract was once used to remove the discomfort of flatulence by checking the bacteria that causes such.

Magical Uses: The Cheyenne tie a piece of the root to a child's necklet, dress or blanket to ward off night spirits.

The Omaha use the leaves as garlands in "mystery ceremonies", as well as chewing the root to ward off sickness.

The Chippewa use a decoction of the root on their fishing nets as a charm.

It is also used in spells for healing, luck, wealth and protection.

Interesting Tidbits: During the Depression, the root was chewed in England as a substitute for tobacco, it kills cravings for nicotine. It is still chewed by Cree elders in Canada to combat fatigue.

If the Calamus of the Bible is the same as this plant, it is a constituent of the anointing oil used by Moses (Exodus 30:22-25).

The leaves were dried and strewn on floors to keep the air sweet-smelling (rushes), even in churches. As it did not grow near London, the importation of Calamus from Norfolk and Suffolk was one of the charges of extravagance brought against Cardinal Wolsey.

According to Gerard, the Tatars (probably those in the Crimea) wouldn't drink water unless they'd first steeped Calamus root in it. Perhaps this was an early form of water purification?

Notes:

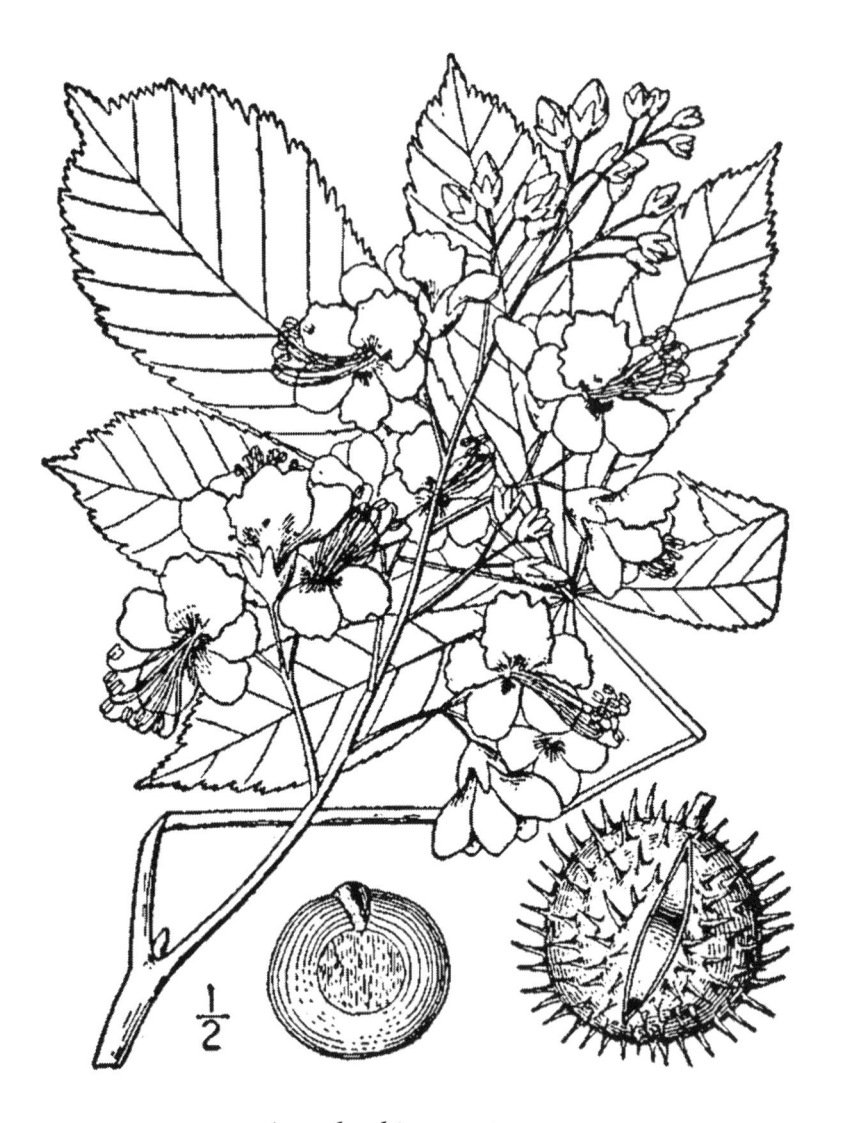

Aesculus hippocastanum

Aesculus hippocastanum
Horse Chestnut, Buckeye

Description: There are approximately 13 Species in the Genus *Aesculus*. The most well-known is a deciduous tree native to Southeastern Europe but cultivated all over the Western hemisphere. It grows from 50 to 80 feet high with widely-spreading branches, grayish-green bark, and has compound, serrated, pointy leaves. The bark of the branches has small, horseshoe-shaped markings, which may be the impetus for the name. White, red or yellow flowers appear in grape-like bunches in May and June. The fruit is a prickly green capsule containing one to six shiny brown seeds (nuts).

Cultivation: It is generally raised from the nuts, sown in early spring. (Store the nuts carefully over the winter – they are susceptible to mold and rot.) The nuts will germinate faster if you soak them in water for a day or so prior to planting. Although Horse Chestnut isn't real picky about its soil, it likes a light, sandy loam best.

Parts Used: Bark and seeds.

Poison: All parts. Toxicity level: III.

Side Effects: The seeds are poisonous if eaten; severe gastrointestinal problems have been seen after ingestion of one seed. (Some sources say roasting destroys this poison.) Other symptoms include reddening of the skin, extreme thirst, diarrhea, hypotension, vomiting, unconsciousness and collapse. Overdosing on medicinal preparations can cause anaphylactic shock. Use of horse chestnut may interfere with anticoagulant medications.

Medicinal Uses: Extracts of the ripe seed are used to treat symptoms of venous and lymphatic insufficiency (varicose veins, hemorrhoids). External creams are used not only for the aforementioned issues but also to treat rheumatism and neuralgia. Seed, leaf or bark tinctures are used as a gargle for mouth ulcers. An infusion of the bark is a tonic, narcotic and febrifuge and has been used in small doses to treat intermittent fevers.

It's thought the Turks used a compound of Horse Chestnut to treat bruising in horses, giving another possible source for the name.

The Iroquois use a compound of the powdered root for chest pains.

Magical Uses: Carrying one of the nuts is thought to prevent and/or heal arthritis. The fruits are also carried for general luck as in a "lucky Buckeye".

Possibly due to the number of seed pods on a tree and then the number of seeds within each pod, Horse Chestnut is used in spells of increase, specifically those for money.

Interesting Tidbits: The dried leaves of Horse Chestnut were used as a tobacco substitute on Guernsey during World War II.

Horse Chestnut seeds were soaked in lime water (to remove bitterness) then dried, ground to a meal and fed to livestock (except pigs, who apparently don't like it) in England during World War I to indirectly increase the amount of grain available for human consumption. (Perhaps soaking them in lime mitigates the poisonous effects because in 1839 it was written, "The Buck-Eye, or American Horse Chestnut, seems to be universally considered in the West a mortal poison;

both fruit and leaves. Cattle affected by it are said to play many remarkable antics, as if intoxicated, turning, twisting and rolling about and around, until death closes their agonies.)

Many, many indigenous cultures (and indeed, today's children all over the world) play games with the nuts, variously known as conkers, oblionker and conqueror.

A. glabra is the state tree of Ohio.

The unbroken nuts may be used as a moth repellant.

Notes:

Aloe ferox, Aloe vera, others
Bitter Aloe, Aloe Vera

Description: The *Aloe* Genus is well-known in the Western world. Although most are native to South Africa, they may be found as ornamentals throughout the world – even in a kitchen window! Aloes are succulents, belonging to the Lily family. While your household Aloe plant may only grow leaves to a length of a foot or so, other Species found in the wild may grow to a height of sixty feet with stems as large as ten feet in circumference.

Cultivation: Aloe is a succulent, like Agave and Cacti and therefore, prefers a very warm climate. Most people grow it as a houseplant where, if it gets enough sun, it does quite well. Aloe is generally propagated by root suckers; or rhizome cuttings but a plant will occasionally have an offshoot called a "pup". This can be carefully divided off the mother plant and repotted. It likes a slightly acidic soil that is well-drained. (If you keep it in a pot, put an inch or two of gravel in the bottom.) Allow the soil to completely dry out before watering.

Parts Used: The leaf gel.

Poison: The aerial portions of the plant *and* the leaf gel. Toxicity Level: II.

Side Effects: The leaf gel is commonly ingested as a laxative. However, high doses (or an overdose by ingesting a small amount for several days) may lead to intestinal bleeding, kidney problems, hypertrophy (fast death) of intestinal tissues and abortion.

Medicinal Uses: Most commonly known as an external application for burns and other skin issues such as dermatitis, eczema, psoriasis, stretch marks and skin ulcers. *However*, it may delay wound healing after surgery. Small doses are ingested for constipation.

Magical Uses: Confers protection: in Africa, the leaves are hung over houses and doors to drive away evil.

Interesting Tidbits: In addition to believing it to be such a miraculous drug that drawings of Aloe on temple walls still exist, the Ancient Egyptians used Aloe to make papyrus-like scrolls. They revered it so highly that an invitation to the funeral of a Pharaoh came with the price of at least one pound of Aloes, and a man's wealth and esteem for the deceased was measured by the number of pounds of Aloes he brought.

Aloes was part of the noxious mixture the Egyptians used for the embalming process.

Even as late as the 1930's (I can find no reference to it today), it was said that Muslims thought the plant a religious symbol: a man who had made the pilgrimage to Mecca was entitled to hang the plant over his doorway, thus conferring the protection of the Prophet to his home.

During the Crusades, the Knights Templar created a drink of Palm wine, Aloe pulp and hemp, calling it "The Elixir of Jerusalem". They believed it added years to their life.

Notes:

Arnica montana
Arnica, Mountain Tobacco, Wolfsbane, Leopardsbane

Description: A perennial plant indigenous to Central Europe, it is found in the higher reaches (usually above 3,500 feet) of Canada, the northern United States and Europe. The slightly hairy, branched stem usually grows 1 to 2 feet high with a flat rosette of oblong leaves. Each plant produces one to nine large, daisy-like yellow flowers, which appear in July or August.

Cultivation: Arnica likes a light, sandy, loamy soil. It can be propagated from seed but grows more easily from root division. Sow seeds after the danger of frost has passed or in a cold frame; divide roots in the spring. Collect roots in the fall, after the stalk has died back.

Parts Used: Flowers and sometimes root.

Poison: All parts of the plant. Toxicity level II.

Side Effects: Taking any part of the herb internally can cause dizziness, heart irregularities and tremors. It may irritate mucous membranes, cause vomiting, or hypotension. Large doses may induce coma and possibly death. Topical application may cause a painful, itchy rash in some allergic people.

Medicinal Uses: For the most part, Arnica is limited to topical use only, due to the toxicity of the sesquiterpene lactones found in all parts of the plant. A homeopathic tincture of the root is used internally for some cases of epilepsy and motion sickness. Homeopathic preparations have also been shown to be effective in some British studies for postoperative swelling, pain and bruising.

External preparations from the flowers (poultices, fomentations, ointments, creams) are effective for bruising, sprains, phlebitis and rheumatoid arthritis.

Magical Uses: In Germany, Arnica was once used to curry favor with the spirits. Bunches of blossoms were gathered at the summer solstice and placed at the corners of the corn fields to ensure a good harvest.

The flowers are added to protection sachets, especially if one is concerned about vampires and werewolves.

Roots of *A. cordifolia* and *A. latifolia* are used by some Native American tribes as love charms.

Interesting Tidbits: It was once thought that application of Arnica tincture to the scalp would make the hair grow.

Notes:

Arum maculatum
Adam and Eve, Cuckoo Pint, Lords and Ladies, Starchwort

Description: The glossy, green-with-purple-blotches leaves grow close to the ground and are some of the earliest to appear in spring. The plant is easy to identify once it puts up the stem, which has a single, hood-like leaf at the very top called the spathe. At the base of the spathe are the male flowers and above them, the female. In the autumn, the lowest ring of flowers forms bright red berries. The leaves, when bruised, give off a very disagreeable odor.

Cultivation: Seeds are best sown in a cold frame as soon as they are ripe. If the seeds are stored, a period of cold stratification may help the germination process. Seeds germinate in one to six months and do best in a sandy soil in shady to partially-shady conditions. Propagation by corm division is best done in the fall.

Parts Used: Root.

Poison: Root Toxicity Level II; Aerial parts and seeds Toxicity Level I.

Side Effects: The berries, while quite attractive, are very acrid. One drop of the juice from the berries will cause a burning sensation in the mouth and throat for hours. This probably discourages a lot more poisonings than there might be, although cramps and convulsion may precede death in the most persistent of children when medical assistance is not immediately available. The juice of the root is also acrid and burning, although drying and cooking takes this effect away.

Medicinal Uses: Even today, the tuber (root) is dried and cooked as one would a potato. It is quite edible and due to the amount of starch, nutritious. The dried root is also powdered and mixed with honey for bronchitis, asthma, flatulence and rheumatism. An ointment is said to be useful for sores and ringworm.

Magical Uses: Mostly used for love magic. The tubers are about the size of walnuts and therefore small enough to carry two on your person to attract love; two sewn into a bag to deflect love; and two given to a newly-married couple to ensure long-lasting love.

Interesting Tidbits: Arum starch was used in Elizabethan times to stiffen the ruffs so fashionable during that period. However, they apparently used fresh root rather than dried: Gerard said it was "most hurtful for the hands of the laundresse that have the handling of it; for it chappeth, blistereth and maketh the hands rough and rugged and withal smarting".

At the same time, a water distillation of the root or the starch itself was used for "beautifying skin" – referring to the whitening of ladies' skin that was fashionable in the 17th century.

Some common names (Lords and Ladies, Adam and Eve) may refer to its resemblance to genitalia – the spadix (stem) being the penis and the spathe the vagina. Gerard knew it as "priests' pintle", pintle being old slang for penis and the fact that it tended to grow around churchyards.

The pollen from the flowers throws off a faint light at dusk.

Notes:

Baptisia tinctoria
Indigo, Wild Indigo

Description: *B. tinctoria* is native to the eastern woods of North America, from Canada down to the Carolinas. It is a perennial with a root that is black on the exterior and yellowish on the interior. It grows up to about three feet high with small, rounded leaves and yellow flowers that appear in late summer, followed by a pea-like pod containing small, bluish-black seeds. While easily found in the wild, it is also grown as an ornamental plant in yards.

Cultivation: It is easily propagated by seed, roots or cuttings. If by seed, scarify and then soak for a day. Experts recommend seeds be started in pots and transplanted to a garden three or four months later. Pieces of root may be taken in either spring or fall. Plant approximately eighteen inches apart in well-drained soil in full sun or partial shade.

Parts Used: Root bark, leaves.

Poison: All, but especially the fruit and seeds. Toxicity Level II.

Side Effects: Low doses will produce vomiting and gastrointestinal disturbances. High doses may produce a burning sensation in the mouth; excessive salivation and perspiration, nausea, hallucinations and paralysis.

Medicinal Uses: A decoction of the root is used as a gargle for mouth problems or a sore throat and as a douche for leucorrhea. A root decoction was once used to treat colds and fever.

Magical Uses: None known.

Interesting Tidbits: As its name implies, the root is used as a blue dye.

Notes:

Berberis vulgaris
Barberry

Description: A well-known shrub, found throughout the majority of the Northern Hemisphere. While native to Europe, northern Africa and some parts of Asia, it can be found cultivated in many gardens as an ornamental. Like most shrubs, it has woody stems growing up to ten feet high, with small leaves that graduate into spines in their second year. The flowers are small and pale yellow, giving way to small, oblong red berries in the fall.

Cultivation: Self-propagates by suckers put out from the main plant but cuttings may be taken in the fall and planted in sandy soil in a pot or cold frame, then transplanted outdoors in the spring. If propagated by seed, fresh are best, especially if you just mash a berry and put it into the ground in the fall, for germination the following spring.

Parts Used: Bark, berries.

Poison: All, especially the bark. Toxicity Level II.

Side Effects: In susceptible individuals, even a normal dose may cause nausea, vomiting and diarrhea. High doses may lead to primary respiratory arrest and lethal kidney damage.

Medicinal Uses: A decoction of the root bark may be used internally in cases of gallbladder problems, jaundice, and as an appetite stimulant. It is also used as a mouthwash for ulcerated gums and for a sore throat. This decoction is very bitter and is generally combined with an aromatic herb to make it more palatable.

Magical Uses: None known.

Interesting Tidbits: The berries have been and are used for garnishing dishes and to make a jelly, as well as being pounded into a flour and used to make a mush by the Yana tribe.

The root, when boiled in lye, yields a yellow dye.

Notes:

Borago officinalis
Borage, Starflower

Description: Originally from the Mediterranean, Borage can now be found naturalized and cultivated in most parts of the world. It is an annual that grows two to three feet tall, has large, wrinkled, deep green leaves and is covered in prickly hairs. The flowers, which generally appear in June to August, are bright blue and star-shaped, giving way to brownish-black nuts.

Cultivation: Borage will grow in virtually any soil. It is easily propagated from rootstock division or seeds sown in early spring. Seedlings should be thinned to about fifteen inches apart. Although an annual, it will readily re-seed itself and appear year after year in the same spot.

Parts Used: Leaves and flowers.

Poison: All parts but especially the flowers. Toxicity Level II.

Side Effects: While Borage was used frequently up to the early part of the twentieth century, we now know that it contains pyrrolizidine alkaloids (PAs), which have mutagenic and carcinogenic properties and it's suggested for external use only. Substantial ingestion of the herb can lead to liver and neurotoxic disorders.

Medicinal Uses: Borage was once used as a refrigerant to bring down fevers and its demulcent qualities were prized for expelling mucus. Despite the PA constituents, it is still used today by naturopathic doctors to regulate metabolism and the hormonal system. It's considered a good remedy for PMS and hot flushes.

Externally, it is used as a poultice for inflammation.

Magical Uses: Perhaps due to the ages-old thought that a drink of Borage would make a man cheerful, and steeped in wine, induce forgetfulness, it's used in a magical tonic to raise spirits and induce courage. Borage will also confer protection.

Interesting Tidbits: Borage seeds are the highest-known plant source of gamma-lineolic acid (GLA) and Borage Oil is a commercial product for GLA supplementation.

The leaves and flowers are still used as vegetables in parts of Germany, Spain, Italy and Greece. They may be found in soup, sauces and as ravioli filling.

Borage leaves have a cucumber-like flavor and were original ingredients in a Pimm's Cup before being replaced by a slice of cucumber or sprig of mint. The flowers are still the traditional garnish.

Notes:

Brassica nigra

Brassica nigra
Mustard (Black)

Description: Its native area is unknown but Mustard was known to the Ancient Greeks. It is now widely cultivated throughout the world for its seeds and seed oil. The plant is an annual, with a branching, angular stem growing from two to seven feet tall. The leaves are alternate and somewhat bristly. Yellow flowers appear from June to November. The seed pods are cylindrical and contain about a dozen small, reddish-brown to black seeds. The seeds have a thin coat which is pitted and no odor, even when crushed; but this changes when they're mixed with water, releasing the volatile oil.

Cultivation: Sow in spring, either broadcast or in drilled holes, a foot or more apart. While not particular about its soil, Mustard suffers easily from overwatering.

Parts Used: Most often the seed but the leaves are used as salad greens.

Poison: All parts but especially the seeds. Toxicity Level: III.

Side Effects: Topical application can cause severe skin irritation, especially in fair-skinned people. Ingestion of large amounts may produce respiratory distress, nausea, vomiting, or diarrhea. Overdose may lead to paralysis of the central nervous system, cardiac and/or respiratory arrest. Livestock poisoning has been reported.

Medicinal Uses: Most often used topically as a poultice to alleviate chilblains, bring down a fever or ease lung congestion experienced with bronchitis or pneumonia. As it is a skin irritant, an application of olive oil after the poultice will feel quite soothing.

In small amounts, Mustard is taken internally to stimulate the appetite.

Magical Uses: Most often seen in fertility or protection spells but may also be used to strengthen mental acuity.

Interesting Tidbits: The Greeks attributed the discovery of Mustard to Asclepius and held it in very high esteem for its medicinal virtues. No one knows when it was first used as a condiment but the Romans, who pounded the seeds and steeped them in wine, probably introduced it to the Saxons. The name comes from "mustum" (the must – newly fermented grape juice) and "ardens" (burning).

Mustard was formerly made up into balls with honey, vinegar and a little cinnamon so it would keep longer. It was then mixed with more vinegar to make a sauce.

Mustard oil is little affected by atmosphere and was highly prized by makers of clocks and other precision instruments.

Notes:

Caulophyllum thalactroides
Blue Cohosh

Description: A perennial native to Canada and the United States, it can be found growing wild in rich, moist soil near swamps and streams. It is a low-growing plant with a simple, erect stem sprouting from a knotty rootstock, producing large tri-pinnate leaves. The yellow-green flowers give way to a pea-sized, dark blue berry.

Cultivation: Prefers full shade and a moist, rich, well-drained soil. Seeds should be scarified prior to sowing and may take up to three years to germinate. Once well-established, the plant will self-sow by sending out runners, yielding a colony that may be divided.

Parts Used: The root.

Poison: All parts but especially the root and seed. Toxicity Level I-II.

Side Effects: In low doses, it may produce vomiting and diarrhea. Higher doses produce a burning sensation in the mouth, excessive salivation and perspiration, uterine contractions, hallucinations, paralysis and respiratory arrest.

Medicinal Uses: Once in favor to treat a multitude of women's problems, as well as rheumatism and epilepsy, its toxicity has led to its fall from grace in the herbal medicine world. Some Native American tribes use it to induce labor and the Cherokee suck on the root sap for toothaches.

Magical Uses: None known.

Interesting Tidbits: Despite known toxicity, the berries were once used as a coffee substitute.

Notes:

Chelidonium majus

Chelidonium majus
Celandine, Greater Celandine, Wart Plant

Description: Either biennial or perennial, Celandine can be found in damp, rich soils in the eastern United States as well as alongside roads or fences and in waste places throughout Europe. The stem is round and slightly hairy, growing from 1.5 to 3 feet tall and branching. At the points where it branches, you will find knobby joints where the twigs will easily break off. The leaves have irregularly lobed leaflets. The bright yellow flowers have four petals arranged like a cross; they appear from late April through September; giving way to narrow, long pods which contain small black seeds. The entire plant has a reddish juice, or latex, that is very bitter and will stain the hands.

Cultivation: Celandine will self-sow (it is actually considered an invasive weed in some parts) but will grow easily from seed in almost any soil, in partial to full sun. Sow seeds after the danger of frost has passed in an area where you will either keep a watchful eye on it or where you don't mind it spreading.

Parts Used: The whole herb.

Poison: All parts. The latex is a powerful skin irritant. Toxicity Level II.

Side Effects: Ingestion of any part of the plant will cause a burning of the mouth, vomiting, paralysis, dizziness, hypotension and possibly collapse. The alkaloids found in Celandine are mildly analgesic and sedative.

Medicinal Uses: Celandine is used today under proper supervision for bronchitis, jaundice and pertussis. A drop of the juice is used for warts and some skin tumors. In earlier times, the juice was used to cure eye ailments; an ointment made from the root was used for hemorrhoids and burns; an infusion of the aerial parts of the plant was used to increase perspiration; and the plant was pounded with vinegar and smeared on the face to get rid of a headache.

Magical Uses: If worn (in a bag to prevent skin contact), it will bring happiness. As well, a piece of the root carried on one's person is said to assist in court cases.

Interesting Tidbits: Pliny says swallows were observed successfully treating chicks' blindness with a drop of the juice from a twig into the chicks' eyes. This legend is said to give the Genus its name from the Greek word for swallow, *Chelidon*.

Notes:

Cinnamomum camphora
Camphor

Description: A native to East Asia and introduced in other parts of the world, it is an evergreen growing to a height of one hundred feet or more with pale bark and glossy, bright green leaves. Masses of small white flowers in the spring give way to bunches of small, berry-like fruit. Cultivated varieties may be found in nearly any sub-tropical climate. It is considered invasive in some parts, and is classed as a Category I invasive in Florida.

Cultivation: Likes a subtropical to tropical climate. In the United States, that means USDA zones 8 and above. Prefers full sun to partial shade and will grow in almost any type of soil. Seed propagation is easiest – directly sow fresh seeds in the fall. Softwood and semi-hardwood cuttings may also be taken in the fall.

Parts Used: Essential Oil, gum (resin).

Poison: The leaves, gum and essential oil. Toxicity Level: II-III.

Side Effects: Ingestion, even in small amounts, may produce excitation and an alcohol-like intoxication. Higher doses lead to vomiting, convulsions, irritation of the stomach lining, and kidney death.

Medicinal Uses: Even though the toxicity of Camphor was known, a small amount of gum, dissolved in olive oil, was once used for heart failure. Today, Camphor (usually the essential oil) is used sparingly and externally only as a rub for sore muscles. Its highly-aromatic properties make it a perfect ingredient in products used externally to clear sinus congestion and may sometimes be found in moth-repellant products.

Magical Uses: Differing opinions: some use Camphor as a love attractant; others use it either for chastity or to deter unwanted affections.

Other sources list Camphor as a cleansing and protective herb, as well as burning the resin or essential oil as a divinatory aid, most notably before bed to assist with true dreaming.

Interesting Tidbits: The essential oil from *C. camphora* trees grown in Madagascar is known as "Ravintsara".

In Australia, *C. camphora* is considered a noxious weed. It crowds out native Eucalyptus trees, which provide food for koalas.

Notes:

Citrus aurantium
Bitter Orange

Description: This tree, a close relative of the Orange we all love as our morning juice (*C. sinensis*), is native to India and China but cultivated anywhere long-term freezing temperatures are a rarity rather than the norm. A small tree with smooth, grayish brown bark, the branches usually spread wide and round until the tree is somewhat globe-shaped. The leaves are oval and evergreen; flowers are whitish. The fruit is somewhat darker than its sweeter relative with a rougher rind.

Cultivation: Propagation by seed is usual but seedlings are available commercially. Plant in full sun (the tree will not grow in full shade) in moist soil. It is tolerant of any type of soil but seems to do best in loam or clay. Do not overwater.

Parts Used: Peel, Essential Oils (from various parts of the plant).

Poison: The peel and essential oils. Toxicity Level II.

Side Effects: Ingestion of the essential oil may lead to violent colic and convulsions. Large doses have led to death in children.

Medicinal Uses: The fruit and peel are used in cookery and alcohol production in various parts of the world; the fruit and leaves are used as a soap. Today, the chief use of this Orange is for its essential oil: *Neroli* is produced from the blossoms, *Petitgrain* from its leaves and young shoots. The Oil of Bitter Orange is used by certified aromatherapists for bronchitis, colds, constipation, flu, poor circulation and as a diuretic.

Magical Uses: It is said the Oil of Bitter Orange (expressed from the peel) may be used for uplifting one's spirit.

Interesting Tidbits: The Bitter Orange tree is very resistant to disease and is used for grafting stock, often the Sweet Orange. The oil is a top note in many perfumes.

Neroli oil, mixed with Vaseline, is used in India as a preventative against leeches.

Notes:

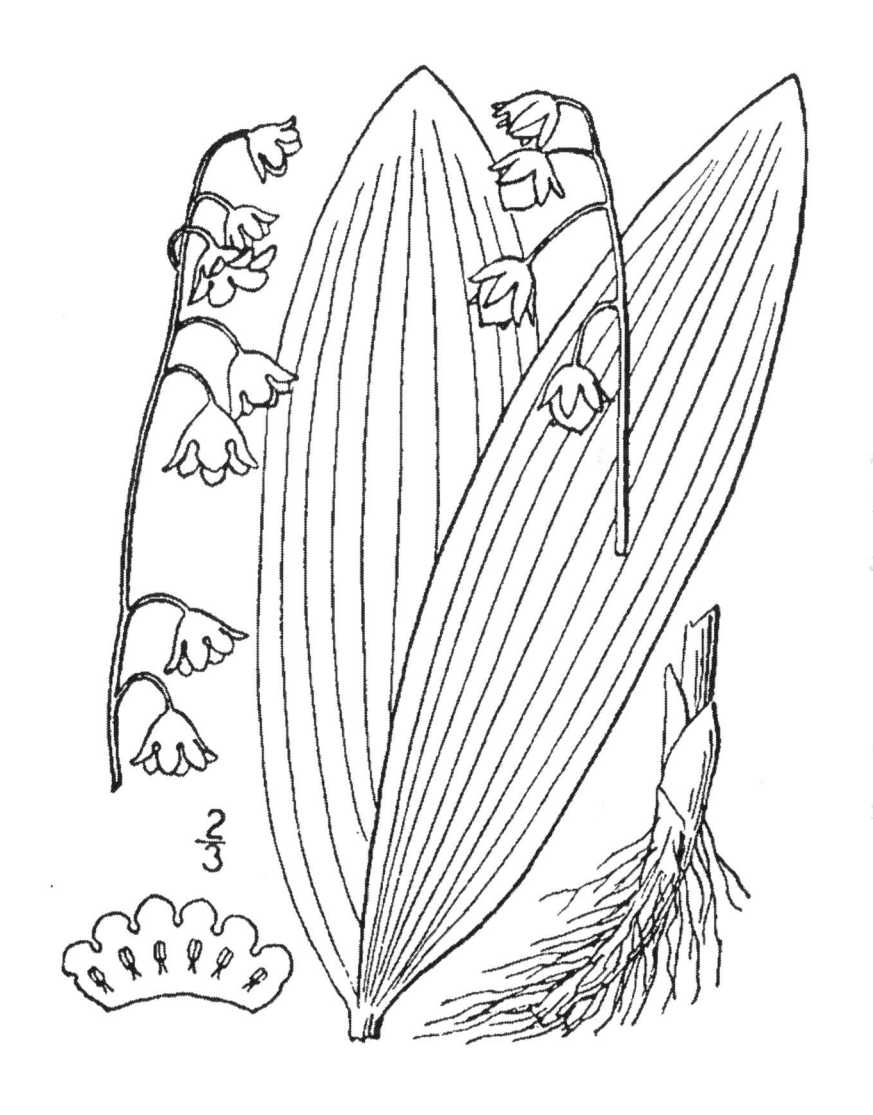

Convallaria majalis

Convallaria majalis
Lily of the Valley, Jacob's Ladder

Description: A perennial plant native to Eurasia, it is grown throughout the world as a garden plant. The root sends up two oblong leaves up to one foot tall. From the base of these leaves the flower stalk appears, with white, bell-shaped flowers drooping from one side. It flowers from early spring through June; then by September the flowers develop into scarlet berries which contain one seed.

Cultivation: Lily of the Valley is easy to cultivate in well-drained, moist soil; preferably in shady conditions. Plant in the fall and augment the soil with rich mulch or manure in the spring, just as growth is appearing. Although it will grow from seed, root division is easiest. It will spread on its own via underground rhizomes.

Parts Used: Aerial.

Poison: All parts of the plant. Toxicity Level I.

Side Effects: Lily of the Valley is a cardiac glycoside, having effects similar to Foxglove. However, it will also produce skin irritation, nausea and exhaustion. Five to ten berries are considered a toxic dose for an adult.

Medicinal Uses: Used under strict supervision to treat congestive heart failure. As late as the 1930's, it was used *rather than* Digitalis to treat many heart "insufficiencies" because its cardiac effects are much milder.

In parts of England, the fresh leaves are bound over cuts and abrasions to speed healing.

The powdered flowers were also used in the past to bring on sneezing, which was thought to bring relief from headaches and earaches.

Magical Uses: Depending on who you speak with, flowers brought into the house will cheer those present *or* will bring bad luck if brought into the house. As well, Lily of the Valley is a symbol of recurring luck in the language of flowers. Even today in France and Belgium, a posy of these flowers is considered a way to wish someone prosperity and happiness. Conversely, in some places in the British Isles, it is considered almost a death sentence to plant the flower, much less gather bouquets or give as gifts. Indeed, it's considered such bad luck that a handkerchief embroidered with a Lily of the Valley was refused as a gift.

Interesting Tidbits: During the Renaissance, a water distilled from the flowers, *Aqua Aurea* (Golden Water) was considered so precious that it was preserved in vessels of gold or silver. This was used for "apoplexy", to strengthen the memory, as a rub for rheumatism and sprains, and various eye complaints.

In theory, the flowers picked before sunrise and rubbed on the face will prevent freckles.

Notes:

Crocus sativus

Crocus sativus
Saffron, Crocus

Description: A small perennial plant, native to Europe. It is mostly cultivated now, in places such as Spain, Italy, France and Iran for the spice. An onion-like corm puts up grayish-green, slightly hairy, skinny leaves, surrounded at the bottom by cylindrical sheaths. In late summer or early fall a funnel-shaped flower appears, which can be any color from white to lilac to reddish-purple.

Cultivation: Corms (bulbs) are planted in mid-summer. It's not too picky about the soil; the climate is more important. It prefers a climate that has rainy springs and dry summers. While irrigation may be necessary in some climates, if the plant is subjected to watering during the flowering season, it will rot. Flowers appear in the fall.

Parts Used: The stigma.

Poison: All parts of the plant. Toxicity Level II.

Side Effects: Saffron is safe in normal cooking amounts but higher doses produce bloody diarrhea, bleeding from the nose and eyelids, and may adversely affect the central nervous system. Higher doses may also induce abortions. (In the James Bond movie, *Casino Royale*, the character Le Chiffre bleeds from the corners of his eyes. That bleeding is explained by the disease hemolacria but perhaps it's due to a saffron overdose instead?)

Medicinal Uses: Saffron has been in use as medicine at least since the time of Hippocrates for just about every ailment imaginable. Strange as it may seem to our modern senses, it was used more in medicine than in cookery but its expense made such use very limited. Of old, nurses and old women would use Saffron tea to promote "eruptions" in diseases such as smallpox and measles. Today, small amounts may help with indigestion. Due to its effects on the uterus, Saffron may be used in cases of dysmenorrhea or amenorrhea.

Magical Uses: A pinch may be added to spells for love, lust, healing, and happiness.

Interesting Tidbits: As the stigmas are what are used, this is a very expensive herb. Approximately 4,320 flowers are required to produce *one ounce* of Saffron.

The stigmas produce a beautiful yellow dye. Saffron is also a symbol of wisdom, light and majesty. For this reason (and probably due to the cost), it was used to dye clothing for royalty and the gods and goddesses of ancient Greece and Rome.

Also in Greece and Rome, it was thought to be a powerful aphrodisiac. Specifically, it increases a woman's libido. There is a Greek myth that the Saffron Crocus sprang up wherever Zeus and Hera made love. Because of this, it was customary in antiquity to strew the marriage bed with the flowers. It still plays a part in the marriage ceremonies of several cultures.

In India, a gold-colored dye was distilled from saffron and this dye was used as an ink to write holy texts. It is associated with the Buddha and his priests still wear saffron-colored robes.

Although sources don't say *what* part of the plant, I am assuming the flowers were strewn in Greek and Roman halls, theaters, bath houses and other places the same way rushes were strewn in northern European cities. For instance, the streets of Rome were strewn with it when Emperor Nero entered the city, and Emperor Heliogabalus swam in a saffron-perfumed pool.

Cornish fishermen believe saffron cakes (pressed-together stigmas) carried on board a ship will spoil the chances of a catch.

Saffron is used to flavor the liqueur Chartreuse.

Saffron bulbs contain twice as much starch as potatoes. During World War I they were used as cattle feed – the spice wasn't in demand anywhere.

Notes:

Cytisus scoparius

Cytisus scoparius
Broom, Scotch Broom

Description: A deciduous shrub native to Europe and naturalized in the United States, particularly in the west. It grows 3 to 5 feet high, has slender, flexible and smooth stems with alternate leaves. Broom produces large, bright yellow flowers in late spring and early summer. These are succeeded by brownish-black pods containing twelve to eighteen seeds. When the seeds are ripe, the pods burst and fling the seeds a fair distance from the mother plant.

Cultivation: It is easily raised from seed, broadcasting them as soon as they are ripe. The roots grow deep, making this an ideal plant for rough soil where nothing else wants to grow. It can also be grown from cuttings taken in the fall and placed in a cold frame over the winter.

Parts Used: Flowering tops.

Poison: All parts of the plant. Toxicity Level II.

Side Effects: Even low doses will produce circulatory collapse, vomiting, sometimes euphoria, paralysis that starts low and works its way up and eventual death from respiratory arrest. There are some reports of hallucinations if smoked like cigarettes. Even in the 18th century, it was known that "its very flowers produce headache, and that the goats which feed on it produce poisonous milk".

Medicinal Uses: Not in use today, although it was once used in compounds with other herbs for cardiac issues and as a diuretic. It also has abortive qualities.

Magical Uses: Effective in spells for causing havoc; may also be used for banishing, purification, and protection.

A Suffolk tradition holds that *If you sweep the house with blossomed Broom in May, you are sure to sweep the head of the house away.*

Interesting Tidbits: Broom is generally thought to be the *Planta Genista* from which the Plantagenet family took its name. It can be seen on the seal of Richard I and decorating the tomb of Richard II in Westminster Abbey. Broom is certainly the badge of Brittany; it is said that Geoffrey of Anjou put a piece of Broom in his helmet at the moment he went into battle.

Before the introduction of Hops, young Broom tops were used to flavor beer – and to make it more intoxicating. Similarly, the seeds were used as a coffee substitute.

Although one would associate Broom with, well, brooms, it's also used for basket-making and thatching cottages and small outbuildings in northern England and Scotland.

Notes:

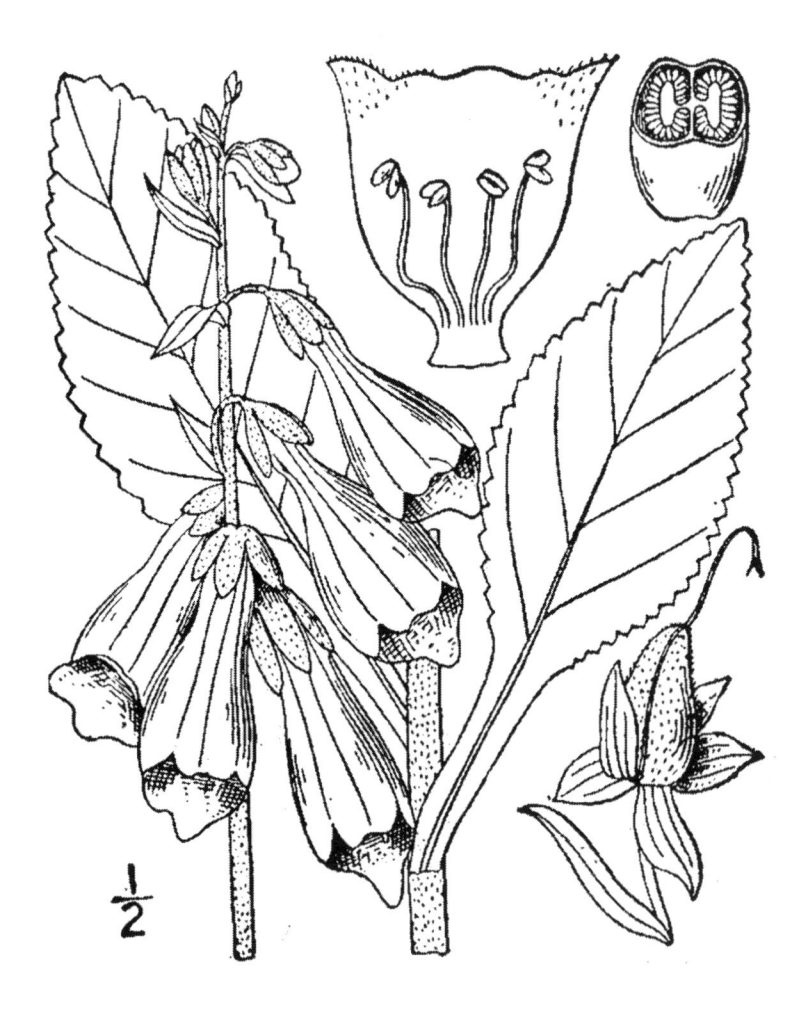

Digitalis purpurea

Digitalis purpurea
Foxglove, Fairies' Petticoat, Fairy Cap, Dead Man's Thimbles

Description: There are 19 Species in the *Digitalis* Genus, all equally toxic. It is usually biennial but will occasionally surprise the gardener by its persistence. Foxglove is a common wildflower in many parts of Europe and North America. It is cultivated in many gardens for its beautiful flowers. The first year will usually only see a rosette of leaves close to the ground. The second year produces at least one, sometimes several tall, succulent stems with long spikes of drooping, bell-shaped rose-to-purplish flowers with spots on the inside. According to experts, the flowers are at perfection in July.

Cultivation: Freely sow in loose soil in the spring and thinly cover. Foxglove is very uncertain in germination; you may need one or more attempts before getting a good patch growing. It likes a mostly-sunny environment.

Parts Used: Leaves.

Poison: All parts of the plant. Toxicity Level I.

Side Effects: Foxglove is a powerful cardiac glycoside. 2-3 dried leaves are toxic to most adults; rapid death arrives via heart failure.

Medicinal Uses: Used since at least 1785 to treat a multitude of heart problems. Due to the uncertain quantity of chemicals in any plant, synthetic Digitalis has taken over from the plant due to its predictability. Herbalists of old also used bruised fresh leaves or an ointment made from them to treat wounds. It is still used externally in the Highlands of Scotland for virtually any skin condition.

Magical Uses: Used in protection spells. How this came about is uncertain.

Interesting Tidbits: Foxglove is favored in murder and/or suicide. Count de la Pommerais poisoned his mistress with digitalis for the life insurance policy. He was guillotined in 1864.

The common name is possibly a corruption of "Folks' glove", the glove of the Good Folk, or fairies. The Genus name, *Digitalis*, is from the Latin *Digitabulum*, a thimble, which the flowers resemble.

One may occasionally find references to Foxglove being unlucky to grow, or forbidden in the house. It was thought that if the flower was inside the house, it would invite witches and/or devils in.

Another tale is told that Foxgloves symbolize war. A Staffordshire man was overheard to say, "[,,,] they mean war. Them Foxgloves is soldiers."

Many Native American tribes use Foxglove as decoration in various ceremonies.

Notes:

Fumaria officinalis
Fumitory

Description: A small annual, this plant is native to Europe (where it may be considered a weed) and naturalized in the United States. It has slender, hollow, sometimes climbing stems; alternate, gray-green leaves; and clusters of yellowish-white to reddish-purple flowers with a reddish-black spot at the tip.

Cultivation: Sow seeds after the last frost in a sunny location. It prefers fertile soil but will grow just about anywhere, as long as it's kept moist. Once established, it will readily self-sow to the point you may want to pull adult plants in the fall before they go to seed to control the population.

Parts Used: The aerial parts.

Poison: All parts of the plant. Toxicity Level: II.

Side Effects: While in general use by herbalists, some susceptible individuals may find it mildly psychoactive, sedative and narcotic. Higher doses may cause a burning sensation in the mouth and throat, nausea, vomiting, diarrhea and hypotension.

Medicinal Uses: Considered a liver tonic and alterative. The infusion is taken internally to treat some skin conditions such as acne and eczema. An infusion may also be used externally to treat conjunctivitis. A renowned Scottish physician, William Cullen (1710 CE-1790 CE), greatly admired an infusion of Fumitory for its ability to remove "moral blemishes": freckles.

Magical Uses: The smoke may be used for exorcism. Indeed, it was used for this purpose in the gardens of St. Gall. It is also used as an aid in money spells.

Interesting Tidbits: One legend says the plant was originally not produced from seed but from vapors rising out of the earth. Pliny says that the juice brings on such a flow of tears that the sight "becomes dim as with smoke".

Notes:

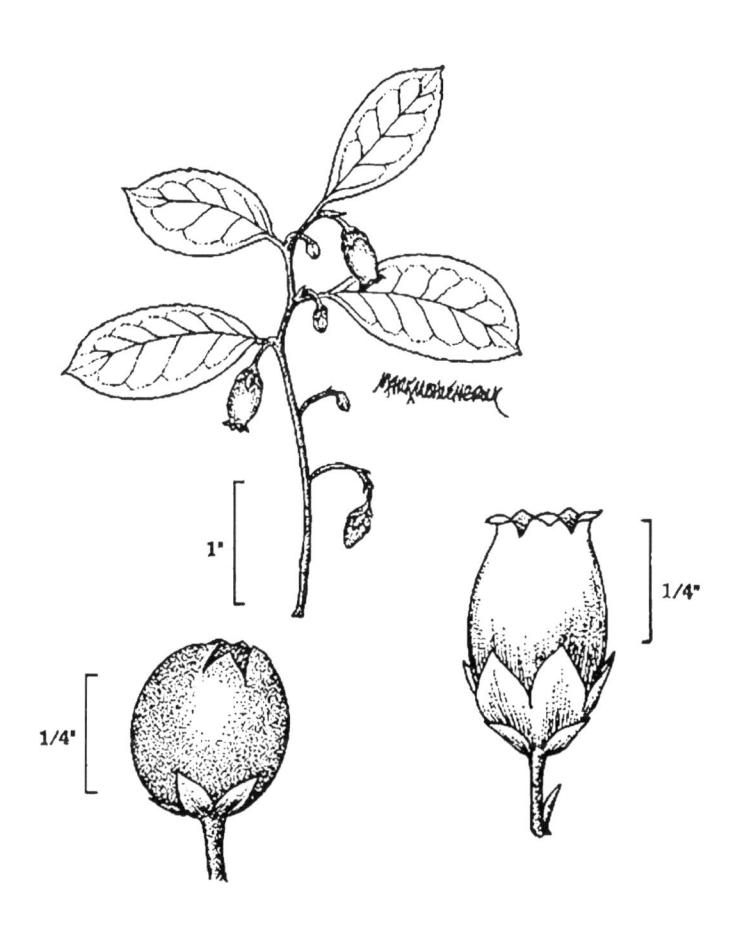

Gaultheria procumbens

Gaultheria procumbens
Wintergreen, Checkerberry, Teaberry, Partridge Berry

Description: A perennial plant native to the eastern part of the North American continent, it is small, creeping and evergreen. It sends up erect branches that grow two to six inches high. The oval, leathery leaves are sometimes hairy along the margins. Solitary, nodding white flowers appear in late summer. Both the leaves and the flowers are at the top of the stem. The flowers give way to red berries.

Cultivation: Prefers woodland-type settings with loamy soil and does best in partial to full shade. It prefers moist but not wet conditions. Cold-stratify the seeds for six to ten weeks, then sow on the surface after the danger of frost has passed. While winter-hardy, it's recommended that you not transplant to their final location until the second year, keeping them in pots or a greenhouse flat until then.

Parts Used: Leaves and essential oil.

Poison: All parts of the plant. Toxicity level II.

Side Effects: External preparations are fine, as is an infusion of the leaves. High doses of infusions or ingesting the essential oil may lead to stomach and kidney damage, and hallucinations. Some people may exhibit allergic reaction in the form of eruptions with skin applications. Salicylic acid is one of the chemicals found in Wintergreen. Those with an aspirin allergy should avoid it.

Medicinal Uses: It's mainly used externally for rheumatism and muscle pain but a refreshing infusion may be made from the leaves. Many Native American tribes use the infusion for headaches, colds, internally to treat rheumatism and general discomfort. Due to its astringent qualities, the Cherokee chew the leaves for dysentery. The fruits are dried and used as food or steeped in brandy as a bitter tonic.

Magical Uses: Placing fresh leaves under one's pillow will confer protection and bring good fortune or place them on your altar to call friendly spirits. Powder the leaves and sprinkle them around the house not only for protection but to break hexes and curses.

Interesting Tidbits: The essential oil is an ingredient in many sweets, chewing gum, dentifrices, root beer and vermouth.

The leaves are dried and smoked as a tobacco substitute.

Notes:

Gossypium spp.
Cotton

Description Approximately 50 Species are in this Genus and they are native to the arid and semiarid areas of the tropics and subtropics. It is a biennial or triennial plant with branching stems up to six feet high and hairy leaves. Different Species have differently colored flowers. The yellow flowers of *G. herbaceum* have a purple spot in the center. The subsequent capsule yields seeds attached to a fluffy tuft – what *we* know as cotton.

Cultivation: Although the plant is either biennial or triennial, it is most often grown as an annual by commercial producers. Cotton requires a long, frost-free period, making it most suitable for subtropical and tropical climates. The soil should be slightly enriched by working in compost before planting when soil temperatures are 60° F or higher on a consistent basis. Plant seeds an inch deep and six inches apart, watering about once a week (more often if conditions are dry) until after the bolls form from the flower. Cotton can also be cultivated as a house plant.

Parts Used: Medicinally, the rootstock. Commercially, the white tuft.

Poison: All parts but especially the seeds. Toxicity Level: II.

Side Effects: In high doses, ingestion may produce gastrointestinal disturbance, internal bleeding, paralysis, cyanosis and death.

Medicinal Uses: A decoction of the root was once used and sold commercially to treat "women's problems". It is well-known as an abortifacient. Oil pressed from the seed is sold commercially as a vegetable oil both on its own and as an ingredient in other preparations, including soap. Unlike other oils pressed from poisonous seeds, this is not heated but "refined, bleached and deodorized" to remove the toxins.

Magical Uses: The tufts (indeed, even 100% cotton fabric) are used in spells for healing, luck and protection. Due to the Genus name, I have used it successfully to stop gossip.

Interesting Tidbits: The use of cotton to make fabric goes back to antiquity. Fragments of fabric have been found in both Mexico and modern-day Pakistan that date back to about 5000 BCE.

We may think of cotton as being white but brown, pink and green are naturally occurring.

When cotton became known as a fiber in medieval Europe, it was thought to come from plant-borne sheep, due to its resemblance to wool. John Mandeville wrote in 1350, "There grew there [India] a wonderful tree which bore tiny lambs on the endes of its branches. These branches were so pliable that they bent down to allow the lambs to feed when they are hungrie."

Notes:

Gymnema sylvestre

Gymnema

Description: Native to the tropical forests of India and Africa, it is a large, climbing vine with elliptical, medium-green leaves. It will root to the ground (or whatever it's climbing on) from nodes on the stalk. It has small, yellowish flowers.

Cultivation: According to one institutional source, standard cultivation practices have not been established. That said, as it's a native to tropical forests, one can assume you'd first need a tropical climate; second, rich soil; and third, shade.

Parts Used: The leaves.

Poison: The leaves. Toxicity Level II.

Side Effects: High doses produce weakness, fever, diarrhea, hypoglycemia, and death by respiratory arrest.

Medicinal Uses: Gymnema has been used for centuries in Ayurvedic medicine as a treatment for diabetes. Chewing the leaves dulls the sense of sweetness and in theory, reduces the craving for sweets. Extracts are sold commercially not only for the treatment of diabetes but for obesity. Science says there's no definitive evidence to support the Ayurvedic claims.

Magical Uses: None known.

Notes:

Hydrastis canadensis
Goldenseal

Description: Goldenseal is a small perennial native to the eastern United States. It can be found in the wild in rich, shady woods and damp meadows, but is more often cultivated. The rootstock is thick, knotty and yellowish in color, with a hairy stem growing up to a foot in height, two five-lobed leaves and a greenish-white flower. The fruit looks similar to a raspberry.

Cultivation: Prefers a rich, loamy, moist soil in partial shade. Seeds aren't considered reliable, therefore, fresh rootstock is generally used. Roots are divided and replanted in the fall and will take two or three years to grow to full size.

Parts Used: The root and rhizome.

Poison: All parts but especially the rhizome. Toxicity Level I-II.

Side Effects: Large doses may cause gastrointestinal disturbance, uterine contractions, and vasoconstriction leading to hypertension. It may act as a central nervous system depressant, producing delirium, hallucinations and cyanosis.

Medicinal Uses: Long known for its antimicrobial and anti-inflammatory properties, Goldenseal is used to treat a variety of conditions from colitis to peptic ulcers. Although the powdered root is sold commercially, it is advisable to take Goldenseal for two to four weeks only; its effects are cumulative and longer use may not only produce toxic symptoms, it may actually cause the problem it was taken to resolve.

Magical Uses: Probably due to the golden color of the root, Goldenseal makes an excellent addition to money spells. It may also be used to promote healing.

Interesting Tidbits: Used by Native Americans for centuries to dye fabric. Several pharmacopeias mention that the saliva will turn yellow if the root is chewed.

Notes:

Laburnum anagyroides (syn. *Cytisus laburnum*)
Laburnum, Golden Chain, Golden Rain

Description: Indigenous to the higher mountains of Europe, Laburnum is cultivated for its flowers. It is a shrub or small tree, often attaining a height of 20 feet or more. Showy, droopy yellow flowers appear in May and June, giving way to a brown or black seed pod containing many seeds.

Cultivation: Plant seeds in a sunny location in late fall. Laburnum isn't picky about its soil but definitely is a sun-worshipper. Cuttings may be taken in early winter. Although it's not a long-lived tree, it will re-seed itself easily.

Parts Used: Inner bark, seeds.

Poison: All parts of the plant. Toxicity Level I.

Side Effects: 3-4 pods (15-20 seeds) are toxic. Even low doses will produce muscular debility, increased pulse, accelerated respiration, sleepiness, and spasms. No human deaths have been recorded from Laburnum poisoning: the body seems to expel the poison and the victim eventually recovers. The twigs and roots are supposedly sweet, tasting something like licorice.

Medicinal Uses: A decoction of the inner bark was once used in small amounts to treat nervous dyspepsia. An extract of the seeds was recommended to treat pertussis and asthma. Due to the poisonous effects of the chemical, *Cytisine,* found in all parts of the plant, it is no longer used medicinally.

Magical Uses: None known.

Interesting Tidbits: The wood, which is quite strong and hard, is used as a substitute for ebony in inlay work and in various other applications where strength and smoothness are indicated.

Notes:

Lobelia inflata

Lobelia inflata
Lobelia, Indian Tobacco, Gagroot

Description: There are approximately 400 Species of Lobelia. *L. inflata* is an annual or biennial plant, native to the northern United States but cultivated in gardens throughout the world. The stem, which grows up to three feet high, is erect, slightly hairy and contains a milky sap. The leaves are light green and hairy. Small blue flowers appear from early summer to first frost.

Cultivation: Seeds can be started indoors or sown outside after the danger of frost has passed. It prefers a moist, rich soil in full sun, although will tolerate partial shade. Once established, it will only require attention in the form of watering if conditions get too dry.

Parts Used: Aerial.

Poison: All parts of the plant. Toxicity Level I.

Side Effects: Similar to those of nicotine poisoning. Chewing fresh leaves produces giddiness, trembling and agitation; smoking produces euphoria. Smaller amounts are a stimulant, large doses are a depressant. Death may occur from respiratory arrest.

Medicinal Uses: Rarely used medicinally but may be added to compounds to treat asthma, bronchitis and pertussis. As late as the mid-19th century, a decoction of the root was administered via the rectum for a strangulated hernia. The Cherokee use a poultice of the root to treat body aches. It was once used to induce vomiting.

Magical Uses: Used in love spells and ceremonies by many Native American tribes. The Iroquois also use an infusion as "anti-love" medicine or the decoction to counteract the sickness produced by witchcraft.

Interesting Tidbits: The herb is named after the French botanist Matthias de Lobel (d. 1616).

The burning plant is used as an insect repellant.

Lobelia was once used as a nicotine substitute. It's possible the chemical constituent *Lobeline* may reduce the effects of nicotine by affecting the brain's production of dopamine. This would lead to its use to treat addictions but has not yet been studied.

A Species of Lobelia, *L. Tupa*, is native to the South American continent and commonly called "The Tupa Poison Plant". From the journal of a Catholic missionary to Chile in the 1700's: "All this plant is a most ready poison; its root yieldeth a deadly milk, as doth also its stem; the odour of its flowers produceth cruel sickness. When one handleth them, care must be had not to bruise them between the fingers; for if one thereafter rubbeth his eyes, some of the milk having to touch them, a man will surely lose his sight, as has been remarked by experience."

Notes:

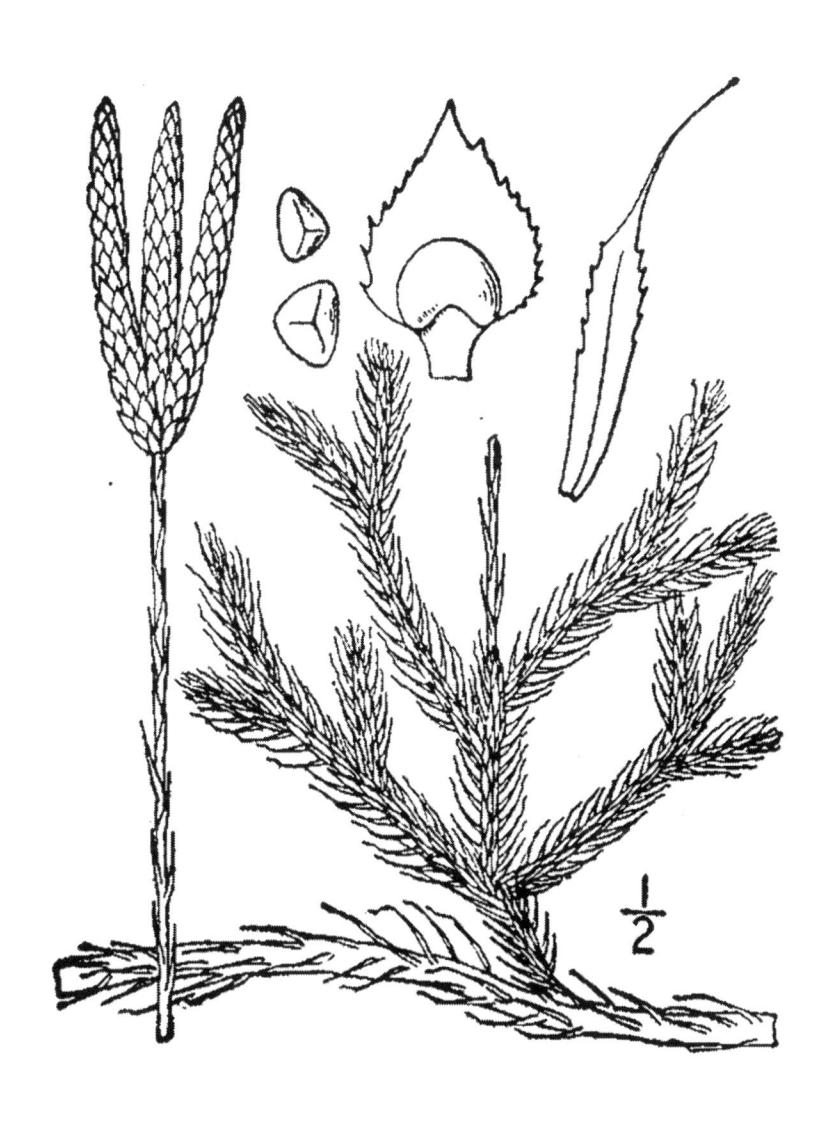

Lycopodium clavatum

Lycopodium clavatum
Club Moss

Description: As Maud Grieve says, this particular Genus occupies an "intermediate place between the Ferns and Mosses". This Species is found throughout the world in dry, coniferous forests and acidic soils. It has creeping, slender stem roots which send up branches with small, stiff leaves tipped with a white bristle. The spores are yellow and appear on one or two club-like spikes at the tip of the plant.

Cultivation: Considered difficult to grow; sow ripe spores on the surface of a rich, sterilized soil. (Potting soil developed for orchids is considered ideal.) Thin or transplant seedlings as soon as they are large enough to handle. Prefers full to partial shade. Keep moist at all times until the plant is fully established.

Parts Used: All except the root.

Poison: All parts of the plant. Toxicity Level: II.

Side Effects: A moderately hazardous neurotoxin, ingestion may produce excessive perspiration, nausea, vomiting, diarrhea, vertigo, speech disorders, and muscular spasms. An allergic reaction to the spores may engender serious conditions of the mucosal membranes.

Medicinal Uses: Indicated for use in cases of gastritis, indigestion and kidney stones but only under professional supervision. A tincture of the spores was once official for treatment of irritability of the bladder.

Magical Uses: Confers protection and power.

Interesting Tidbits: The spores have been used as a binder in the manufacture of pills and as a dusting agent on condoms.

Because they are easily flammable, the spores were used as flash powder for photography and may still be found as explosive material in fireworks.

If you were to coat your hands with Club Moss spore powder, they'd stay dry when dipped in water. They were the original dusting powder used for fingerprint detection.

Notes:

Malus domestica (syn. *Pyrus malus*)
Apple

Description: Need I complete this section? Okay. The original wild ancestors of this plant may be found in the mountains of Central Asia but it has been cultivated throughout the world for thousands of years. The Apple is a small, deciduous tree, reaching from ten to thirty-nine feet tall with a broad, dense crown. The leaves are small and serrated, with a slightly-downy underside. The flowers are generally pinkish-white and appear in the spring. The fruit matures in autumn. There are more than 7,500 known cultivars of this popular fruit.

Cultivation: Wild apples generally grow from seed but production plants are cultivated by grafting. They prefer a loamy soil and full sun; most cultivars are hardy in USDA zones 3 to 8 but check before purchasing. Apples do not self-pollinate so you will need at least two varieties for cross-pollination. They are prone to insects, fungus and bacterial infections. Apple cultivation is not for a lazy person!

Parts Used: The fruit.

Poison: The seeds. Toxicity Level: II.

Side Effects: Crushing the seed releases a form of cyanide which inhibits cellular respiration. In high doses: vomiting, increased respiration, headache and possibly respiratory and cardiac arrest.

Medicinal Uses The malic and tartaric acids in apples will neutralize the acid products of gout and indigestion and will help digest other foods. Peeled and grated unripe apples will ease diarrhea while ripe apples have a laxative nature. Eating a whole apple is good for the teeth: it helps clean off deposits while pushing the gums back.

Magical Uses: In Ancient Greece, the Apple was sacred to Aphrodite and has long been used in love spells. The blossoms may be added to sachets, potions and incense. The fruit has been used in love divination: cut the apple in half and count the number of seeds. If even, marriage will soon occur. Beware: cutting one of the seeds will bring a stormy relationship; two or more means widowhood.

One that I remember from my youth: as you peel an apple, recite the alphabet. When the peel either breaks or is completely removed, the letter you're on will be the first letter of the first name of your "true love". I'm not sure this spell works. My grandmother was a whiz at peeling an apple in one continuous spiral and my grandfather's name started with 'A'. I, on the other hand, after all these years of making pie, still can't manage more than a turn or two before the peel breaks and my beloved's name starts with 'P'.

It is also an ingredient in healing spells.

The Norse Edda implies that apples will confer immortality: the goddess Idunn provided apples to the gods to give them eternal youthfulness.

The Apple is also associated with fertility in Norse mythology: several chapters of the Edda relate the Apple to pregnancies.

Interesting Tidbits: In the 7th century BCE, apples were so expensive in Attica, Greece, that bridal couples had to share one on their wedding night.

In some periods of the settlement of the American Midwest, settlers were required by law to plant orchards of apples and pears in order to uphold the right to the claimed land.

The larynx of the human throat has been called "Adam's Apple" because someone thought it was caused by the forbidden fruit of the Bible (variously interpreted as an apple or a pomegranate) sticking in Adam's throat.

Notes:

Mentha pulegium
Pennyroyal

Description: This is the smallest Species of the Mint family. It is a native of most of Europe and parts of Asia. It has weak, prostrate stems up to three feet in height but you'll generally find it crawling rather than standing. The leaves are grayish-green and hairy; clusters of bluish to purplish flowers appear at the nodes in mid-summer.

Cultivation: Like nearly any Mint, sow seed in full sun to partial shade after the danger of frost has passed. Keep moist but not wet and germination will occur quickly. While it will survive dry conditions, the quality of the herb and essential oil will drop off. Pennyroyal will also easily root itself from stem nodes. These plants can then be divided off in spring or fall. Also like the rest of its Family, it will quickly spread and take over an area.

Parts Used: Aerial portions.

Poison: All parts of the plant. Toxicity Level II.

Side Effects: Ingestion of the infusion may prove to be slightly narcotic. Higher doses produce vomiting, diarrhea, hypertension, abortions and death through respiratory arrest. Ingestion of as little as one ounce of the essential oil has also been reported to be fatal.

Medicinal Uses: Apart from its well-known use as a flea repellant, Pennyroyal has a long history of treating a multitude of women's problems, especially heavy periods. It has been used, as well, to treat flatulence. Pliny had an even longer list of conditions for which Pennyroyal was a supposed remedy and thought it more healthful in some cases than roses.

Magical Uses: Pennyroyal is an excellent herb to use to magically prevent many types of stomach ailments; to "clear the air" after an argument; and is very useful for business people who travel a lot: place a leaf in the shoe to avert travel fatigue and as an aid to all business negotiations.

Interesting Tidbits: The Species name *pulegium* is given by Pliny due to its powers of driving away fleas, *pulex*. Maud Grieve tells us that one of its common names is *Pudding*

Grass, from being used as stuffing in hog's puddings. One famous recipe included Pennyroyal, Pepper and Honey.

One of the books of Albert Magnus mentions Pennyroyal: "by putting drowning flies and bees in warm ashes of Pennyroyal, they shall recover their lyfe after a little tyme and by ye space of one houre and be revived".

Notes:

Momordica charantia
Balsam Pear, Bitter Melon

Description: A native to Eastern India, this is a climbing annual that has made its way to the rest of the tropical and subtropical parts of the world. It is an annual, climbing vine, growing fifteen feet and longer, with three-to-seven lobed leaves, alternating on the vine. The plant bears separate male and female flowers, which in the Northern Hemisphere appear in June or July, followed by fruit in September to November. The fruit looks rather like a mutated cucumber, sometimes dark green, sometimes gray and very warty in appearance.

Cultivation: Favors warm to hot weather. Seeds should be soaked overnight before planting. It prefers full sun and rich soil, native gardeners suggest a location along a riverbank. Keep the plant moist not only during germination but for the whole growing season.

Parts Used: In cookery, the fruit. In medicine, the juice.

Poison: The seeds and rind of the ripe fruit. Toxicity Level I.

Side Effects: Ingestion of the seeds or rind leads to severe and possibly fatal vomiting and diarrhea. The fruit is also considered an abortifacient.

Medicinal Uses: Bitter Melon has been used for centuries in various cultures for stomach complaints, to prevent and treat malaria and as an antiviral against diseases such as chickenpox and measles. The juice is currently being suggested as a treatment for diabetes. (My textbook says to "hold your nose and down a shot [one ounce] twice a day".) Researchers are currently studying an extract that may kill breast cancer cells.

Magical Uses: None known.

Notes:

Myristica fragrans
Nutmeg, Mace

Description: Nutmeg is the seed inside the fruit; Mace is the aril surrounding the seed. Nutmeg is a tree native to Indonesia and cultivated in the West Indies, South Africa and other tropical climates. The tree will grow up to 25 feet tall and has a grayish-brown, smooth bark. The leaves are dark green and glossy on top, paler green below. The tree will not flower until around nine years old. Flowers give way to the fruit – a brown, wrinkled, oval drupe containing a kernel covered by a bright red membrane, or aril.

Cultivation: *Requires* a tropical climate. Many farmers increase their trees by replanting volunteers – those plants grown from seeds dropped by the trees. *Fresh* seeds are required if cultivating from seed and one must differentiate male from female seeds. Both are required for cross-pollination. Young trees require both windbreaks and protection from the sun.

Parts Used: Essential oil, seed, aril.

Poison: The essential oil, seed and aril. Toxicity Level II.

Side Effects: Ingestion may produce stomach cramps, flatulence and catarrh. It is also mildly hallucinogenic but along with the hallucinations may come headaches, stomach pain, double vision, delirium, heart palpitations and tachycardia. As few as two whole nuts may cause death.

Medicinal Uses: Both dried nutmeg and mace are used in cookery. Avicenna (c. 980-1037 CE) is said to be the first to notice the medicinal properties of Nutmeg. Nutmeg is rarely used alone but may be added to compounds for flatulence and to correct the nausea arising from other drugs. A nutmeg infusion was used in the 19th century to treat insomnia.

Magical Uses: A nutmeg is either carried in the pocket or threaded and tied to braces (suspenders) to prevent or cure rheumatism. The same is done for general luck and the powder is included in many spells for money or luck.

Interesting Tidbits: Nutmeg was a popular but expensive spice in the 17th to 19th centuries. It was fashionable among the wealthy and one can't talk about nutmeg, even historically, without talking about the hallucinogenic qualities that some folks (who could afford it) liked. It was so popular that the Dutch massacred the people of the Banda Islands in 1609 to gain control of their nutmeg trade.

The Dutch and British were chasing each other all over the world during the 17th century in attempts to control the spice trade. Nutmeg was so important that in 1667, the Dutch traded the island of Manhattan in exchange for a nutmeg-producing island and South American sugar-producing territory controlled by the British.

Did I say it was expensive? In said 19th century, the lady of the house would carry a silver grater and nutmeg box on her chatelaine (a belt or loop worn at the waist with items needed to run a household) ... probably right next to the house keys.

Notes:

Phaseolus lunatus
Lima Bean, Butter Bean

Description: Native to Central and South America, the Lima Bean figures in both Andean and Mesoamerican cultures, and is thought to have been domesticated around 2000 BCE. By the 1300's CE, cultivation had spread north of the Rio Grande and somewhere in the 1500's, it found its way to Europe. It's a perennial plant, either bush-or pole-style, with pinnate leaves, white flowers and broad, flattened pods. The pod contains several white or pale green seeds, depending on the type.

Cultivation: If you don't start them indoors, sow seeds outside *well* after the danger of frost has passed – you want soil that is consistently 65° F or above. While they will grow in partial shade, full sun will produce a more abundant harvest. They prefer a loose, well-drained soil that is rich, but avoid planting with fresh compost. Depending on your climate (and whether you grow bush or pole beans), you may be able to get two or more crops in one growing season, especially if you sow succession crops about every two weeks.

Parts Used: The seeds.

Poison: The seeds. Toxicity Level II.

Side Effects: Lima beans must be cooked and served without their cooking water to eliminate the toxins. Improper preparation leads to symptoms typical of cyanide poisoning: flushed face, heavy breathing, headache, and in severe cases, respiratory and cardiac arrest.

Medicinal Uses: They are an excellent source of dietary fiber and protein. Due to the fiber content, eating Lima Beans helps regulate blood sugar and cholesterol levels, and aids in the prevention of constipation.

Magical Uses: None known.

Interesting Tidbits: The common name "Lima Bean" derives from the label on the shipping boxes indicating origin: "Lima-Peru".

Notes:

Phytolacca americana

Phytolacca spp.
Pokeweed, Inkberry

Description: There are approximately 25 Species in the *Phytolacca* Genus but the most well-known is *P. americana.* It is native to North America but also found in other parts of the world. A four- to twelve-foot stem may be as large as an inch in diameter. The stem is light green when young, purplish-green later. The leaves are oblong and dark green. White or greenish-white flowers appear in mid- to late-summer, followed by a deep purple berry.

Cultivation: Generally doesn't need to be cultivated: it's considered a weed and will self-sow. However, soak the seeds in cold water for a few days, changing the water every day. Plant two to three times as many seeds as you want plants; it doesn't germinate easily. Germination takes one to two months in moist soil. Prefers full sun but will easily tolerate light shade, especially in a woodland setting.

Parts Used: Root.

Poison: All parts of the plant except very young leaves. Toxicity Level II.

Side Effects: Nausea, vomiting, abdominal pain, headaches, circulatory problems. Individuals may also experience narcotic-like symptoms such as sleepiness. The sap is an eye irritant. Overdose of medicinal preparations is the most common form of poisoning.

Medicinal Uses: The young shoots and leaves are eaten in a fashion similar to asparagus and other spring greens. It's most commonly used as a laxative or purgative (some 18th century physicians proposed that it be used as a substitute for Ipecac) but may help laryngitis and the mumps in some instances. The dried root is used in ointments for skin diseases such as psoriasis but will cause smarting and heat upon application. It was once used as a cancer remedy.

A Chinese relative, *P. acinosa*, is used to treat apoplexy. The fresh leaves of this plant are reported to have antiviral properties.

Magical Uses: An infusion of the root either sprinkled around the house or used in a bath will break hexes. The Iroquois use the entire plant for bewitchment.

Interesting Tidbits: The juice of the berries makes a wonderful ink all on its own, or as a red stain for skin adornment.

At one time, the juice of the berries was used to enhance the color of port wine but this practice was discontinued because it was found to spoil the taste of the wine.

Notes:

Podophyllum peltatum

Podophyllum peltatum
American Mandrake, May Apple

Description: Five Species are native to many parts of North America. The rootstock produces a simple round stem, one to two feet high, forking at the top and crowned with large, smooth leaves arranged somewhat like an umbrella. A single white, waxy flower appears at the fork, usually in May. The flower falls off and a yellow fruit bearing a resemblance to a rosehip appears.

Cultivation: Prefers moist soil in partial shade. Although it can be found wild in woods throughout most of the eastern United States, it will easily grow from seed. Plant in moist soil in the fall for emersion in the spring. Seedlings also transplant easily. Root division is the easiest method of cultivation – all parts of the root will grow.

Parts Used: Root.

Poison: All parts of the plant except the root and mature fruit. Toxicity Level I.

Side Effects: Ingestion may lead to strong irritation of the mucous membranes, abdominal pain, vomiting, diarrhea, tachycardia, damage of the central nervous system, delirium, coma and possible death from respiratory arrest.

Medicinal Uses The fully dried root is used in small doses along with a corrective herb such as licorice in cases of constipation. The juice of the berry is used to cure warts.

Chemicals found in *Podophyllum* are converted to chemotherapeutic agents and used in the treatment of testicular cancer and lymphoma.

Magical Uses: Used in love charms by the Delaware Indians.

Interesting Tidbits: The fruit is toxic when green, quite edible when ripe.

A decoction of the plant is sprayed on potato plants to kill potato bugs.

Notes:

Pulsatilla vulgaris
Pasque Flower, Meadow Anemone, Dane's Blood

Description: Found wild in dry areas of most every country in Central and Northern Europe, Pasque Flower is a small perennial plant with hairy stems. The flowers, which generally appear before most of the leaves, are single, about 1½ inches across and purplish-blue (although some variants produce white or red flowers). The seed vessels are small, brown and hairy, with long, feathery tails.

Cultivation: Pasque Flower prefers full sun and well-drained, neutral-to-alkaline soil. Sow outside in the autumn, or start in a cold frame over the winter months. The seeds will germinate more easily if cold-stratified before planting. Because of the lightweight seeds with "feathers" that are easily windblown, Pasque Flower will readily re-seed itself, many times where you didn't originally plant it. Young, smaller plants can be transplanted; older ones have a longer taproot that makes them difficult to move.

Parts Used: The aerial portion of the plant.

Poison: All parts of the plant. Toxicity Level II.

Side Effects: Severe, allergic dermatitis when any part of the fresh plant comes in contact with the skin. Ingestion may produce gastrointestinal disturbance, nephritis and paralysis of the central nervous system. The toxic principles rapidly degrade with drying.

Medicinal Uses: A tincture or fluid extract is used to allay coughs associated with asthma, bronchitis and pertussis. It may also be used in the relief of headaches, neuralgia and some symptoms of PMS.

Magical Uses: Not in great use magically, but may be added to spells for health, healing and protection.

Interesting Tidbits: The juice of the flowers will yield an impermanent green stain to paper and natural fabrics. It has been used to color Easter eggs.

Gerard gave it the name "Pasque Flower" or "Easter Flower" because of the time of blooming (April to June).

One legend says Pasque Flowers sprang up in places that had been soaked by the blood of Romans or Danes (hence "Dane's Blood") because they often appear on barrows or boundary banks.

Notes:

Rhamnus cathartica
Buckthorn

Description: There are approximately 135 Species in the *Rhamnus* Genus. The Latin *cathartica* comes from the Greek *kathartikos*, meaning "cleaning" or purging. This particular plant is a deciduous, woody, branched shrub rising to 10 or 12 feet with smooth, brownish-black bark on the stem and lighter bark on the twigs. Prominently-veined, finely-tooth leaves gather in clusters on the spiny branches. The flowers are small, yellow and appear in bunches, followed by small berries that are green and change to black when ripe. Although indigenous to North Africa, it may be found throughout Europe and northern Asia, as well as a cultivated ornamental shrub in other parts of the world.

Cultivation: Separate the seeds from the fruit as soon as ripe (usually around September) and plant almost anywhere. As with most woody plants, it may also be propagated by root cuttings planted in the fall. It is shade-tolerant and will grow moderately fast but is short-lived. Caution: Buckthorn is considered an invasive Species in many parts of the world because its shade prevents native plants from growing. Ensure your locality doesn't consider it such.

Parts Used: Berries (other Species, the dried bark).

Poison: The bark and berries. Toxicity Level II.

Side Effects: Excessive ingestion of the berries can lead to death from serious diarrhea.

Medicinal Uses: Dried berries were used in traditional medicine as a blood purifier and diuretic. It is still used today as a laxative. The bark of other Species in the *Rhamnus* Genus is also used as a laxative.

Magical Uses: Considered by many to be a good luck charm: string the dried berries and carry or wear as a necklace. Placing the spiny branches at windows or doors will confer protection on a room or an entire house.

Interesting Tidbits: The unripe berries will produce a yellow dye; the ripe ones, mixed with Gum Arabic and limewater, yield a green pigment known as "Sap or Bladder

Green", a favorite of watercolor artists. The bark will also yield a yellow dye.

Buckthorn was well-known to the Anglo-Saxons and is mentioned in herbals dated to before the Norman Conquest. Welsh physicians of the thirteenth century prescribed a drink of Buckthorn boiled with honey as an appetite stimulant.

Notes:

½

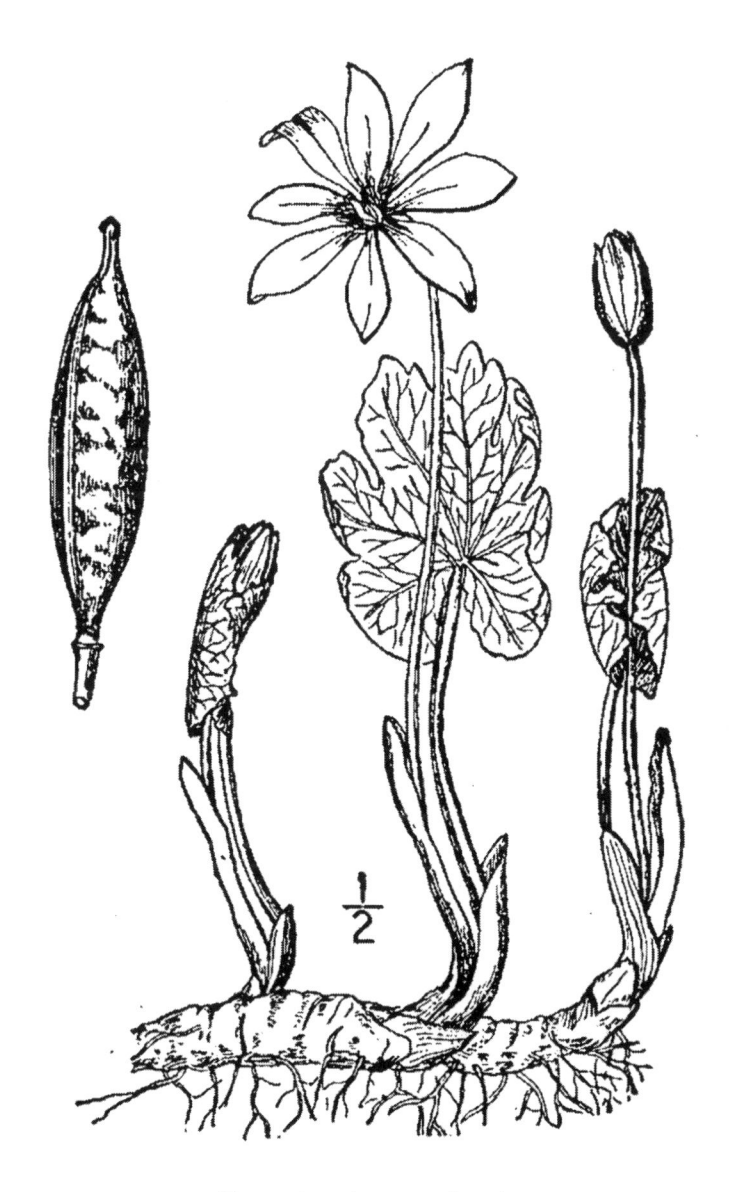

Sanguinaria canadensis

Sanguinaria canadensis
Bloodroot, Indian Paint

Description: A native of North America, this is a monotype Genus, meaning it's a one-of-a-kind plant. It is a stemless perennial with lobed leaves and white, waxy flowers. The leaves grow larger after flowering. The seed is an oblong pod about an inch long. All parts of the plant produce a red latex.

Cultivation: The seed is rarely available but Bloodroot will readily grow from rhizomes split off the main plant. Do this in spring before the flowers appear or in the fall when the plant has died back. It prefers rich, moist soil with full sun.

Parts Used: The root.

Poison: The leaves and root. Toxicity Level II.

Side Effects: Even small doses of an extract may have narcotic effects; this is easily achieved by handling the plant without gloves and allowing the juice to absorb through the skin. Higher doses may produce convulsions similar to strychnine poisoning, excessive salivation, enhanced nerve sensitivity followed by paralysis of those same nerves and death by respiratory arrest.

Medicinal Uses: It is traditionally used as an emetic, expectorant and antispasmodic to treat various ailments of the respiratory tract. It is still found in small amounts as an ingredient in commercial cough syrups. Sanguinaria has anti-plaque activity and is sometimes found in dental products such as toothpaste and mouthwashes.

Magical Uses: Worn or carried, the root will confer protection or attract love. Used in purification spells.

Interesting Tidbits: The root has long been used by Native Americans as a red dye for both bodies and clothing. American and French fabric makers also used the root as a dye.

Notes :

Sassafras albidum (syn. *Sassafras officinale*)
Sassafras

Description: Sassafras is a Genus with three Species. A deciduous tree native to eastern North America and eastern Asia, Sassafras grows up to 60 feet tall and may spread to 40 feet in diameter. The bark of the young tree is smooth and orangish-brown, becoming deeply furrowed and reddish-brown when mature. The leaves are alternate, somewhat furry on the underside and have varying shapes from oval to entirely three-lobed. Tiny yellow flowers appear in spring; male and female flowers are found on separate trees. The fruit, which is blue-black and pea-sized, matures in late summer. All parts of the tree are extremely fragrant: the young leaves and twigs will produce a citrus-like scent when crushed.

Cultivation: Found wild in open woods, along fences and in fields. It is often planted as an ornamental. It will tolerate a variety of soils but prefers moisture and good drainage.

Larger trees will be found in more southern climates where temperatures are warmer and rainfall is plentiful.

Parts Used: Bark, root bark.

Poison: The wood and essential oil. Toxicity Level II.

Side Effects: High doses may produce nephritis, unconsciousness, weakness. Ingestion of the oil may produce death by paralysis of the respiratory system. The primary chemical constituent, safrole, is considered to be mutagenic and carcinogenic. Liver damage has been reported.

Medicinal Uses: Widely used by Native Americans and white men alike, Sassafras enjoyed a reputation as a cure for gonorrhea and syphilis. It is anodyne, antiseptic, diaphoretic, diuretic and a stimulant. As such, it was used to bring down fevers, promote perspiration, as a wash for sore eyes, and recommended to treat gout, rheumatism, arthritis and skin problems. The Cherokee also used it to treat high blood pressure, the Seminole as an antidiarrheal. Sassafras tea was drunk as a spring tonic and even produced commercially in London under the name "Saloop" until the early part of the 20th century.

Magical Uses: A decoction of the bark was used by many Native Americans to purify oneself and ward off evil spirits after funerals or by doctors after the death of a patient. It may be placed in the wallet to attract money or used in healing spells.

Interesting Tidbits: The name "Sassafras" is said to have been applied by the Spanish botanist Nicolas Monardes in the 16th century. Supposedly, it's a corruption of the Spanish word for Saxifrage (Saxifraga).

At one time in the 16th century, exportation of Sassafras from the Colonies to England was second only to tobacco in quantity.

Sassafras makes an excellent fire starter due to the flammability of its natural oils.

The leaves are used in Creole cuisine as a condiment in sauces. They are dried and ground and may be found in stores as Filé Powder or Gumbo Filé.

Once an ingredient in root beer, Sassafras oil was banned by the FDA in 1960; the commercially-produced root tea just a couple of years later due to the carcinogenic nature of safrole. The root extract (with the safrole removed) was finally approved in 1994 and is still a favorite ingredient of microbrewers.

It is sometimes found as an ingredient in incense and soaps favored by the Cherokee.

Notes:

Simmondsia chinensis
Jojoba

Description: Native to the southwestern United States and northwestern Mexico, Jojoba is a perennial, evergreen shrub-to-tree that grows up to fifteen feet high and can be just as wide. The leaves are oval, gray-green, about 1.5 inches long and rather waxy-looking. Flowers are small, greenish-yellow; female flowers are smaller and paler while male flowers are larger and yellower. Male and female flowers are borne on different plants although some hermaphrodite plants have been found. The fruit is a green capsule with up to three seeds, which resemble coffee beans. Fruit generally doesn't appear until the fourth year. The oil, which is actually a liquid wax, is approximately 50% of the seed's dry weight.

Cultivation: Plants are damaged when temperatures fall below 20°F; frost will reduce yield in even mature plants. Therefore, a fairly warm, semi-arid climate is preferable with light or medium textured soil. Seeds may be germinated in warm vermiculite or sand and transplanted when the seedlings are 6-12 inches tall. Direct-seeding is best when soil temperatures reach 70°F. Plant seeds one inch deep, 12 to 18 inches apart and keep moist (but not wet).

Parts Used: The oil.

Poison: The seeds. Toxicity Level II.

Side Effects: Reports of contact dermatitis exist but ingestion of the seeds and/or oil has not been studied in humans. It is known that ingestion of the seed meal caused reversible depression of red blood cells in rats. Erucic acid (14% of jojoba oil) is known to cause myocardial fibrosis.

Medicinal Uses: While chiefly used in cosmetic and hair care products, jojoba oil has been used externally by the natives of the American Southwest and northern Mexico for muscle aches, skin irritations and burns. Internally, a coffee-like beverage was taken to treat colds, sore throats and indigestion. Due to the anti-inflammatory properties of the myristic acid in jojoba, it is gaining popularity for the treatment of psoriasis, eczema and rheumatism.

Magical Uses: None specifically known but it makes an excellent base oil: as it's actually a liquid wax, it won't go rancid as fast as other, more volatile oils.

Interesting Tidbits: The Latin for the Species, *chinensis*, was an accident. The botanist John Link misread the collection label "Calif" as "China".

Jojoba has been used to prevent desertification in the Thar Desert in India.

Jojoba has been proven as an alternative industrial oil and a replacement for non-renewable fossil fuel.

Notes:

Solanum tuberosum
Potato

Description: Ah, the lowly potato. Who doesn't know the tasty and nutritious tuber that graces tables around the world? What you may not know is that the potato grows wild throughout the Americas and is thought to have been domesticated in Peru and Bolivia more than 7,000 years ago. It is an herbaceous perennial that grow about two feet high, bearing flowers that are white, pink, red, blue or purple, depending on the variety. After flowering, some varieties will produce small, green fruits that resemble cherry tomatoes (which can be toxic). What we eat is actually a tuber – a swelling on a root where the plant stores starches.

Cultivation: Some varieties are grown from true seed but most people can produce a successful crop by planting cut-up tubers that include at least one or two "eyes" (which will become sprouting rootlets). They can also be propagated by cuttings. While not picky about the type of soil, it must be very loose and as weed-free as possible. Tubers will not form if the soil temperature reaches 80°F, so they are considered a cool-season crop. Indeed, most of the potato production in the United States is in northern states and mostly in Scotland in the UK. Since new tubers may form at the soil surface and exposure to sunlight leads to the greening of skins, it's important to ensure you either mound the dirt or cover with plastic or a dense mulch. They need to be kept moist but not wet. As with the majority of the *Solanums*, potatoes are very susceptible to pests.

Parts Used: The tuber.

Poison: All green parts. Toxicity Level II.

Side Effects: Ingestion of the green parts of the plant (or the green skin of a tuber exposed to sunlight) may lead to vomiting, internal bleeding, excessive salivation, headache, delirium, fever and coma. In severe cases, death occurs by respiratory arrest.

Medicinal Uses: Widely used as a foodstuff. The skin, with honey applied, is a folk remedy for burns in India. Raw potato juice is drunk for the treatment of gout, rheumatism and lumbago, as well as applied externally (either a poultice or fomentation) for sprains and bruises. Should you burn yourself, applying a fresh cut potato will ease the sting quickly.

Magical Uses: A raw potato was carried in the pocket to ward off rheumatism. The tuber is useful in making poppets or using simply the "eyes" in poppet-making. The Cherokee took an infusion of the leaves to "relieve loneliness due to death in the family".

Interesting Tidbits: "Seed potatoes" are not those that actually produce seeds; they're the tubers or pieces of tubers with eyes.

The potato was introduced to England in 1586 by Sir Walter Raleigh, who brought it back from Virginia. For several hundred years, it was considered a delicacy. In the time of James I (1566-1625), potatoes cost two shillings per pound (approximately $9.70 in current US dollars).

Although introduced to Spain from Peru early in the 16th century, it took much longer to gain popularity on the Continent. For some reason, they were banned in Burgundy during the 16th century because it was feared frequent consumption would cause leprosy.

Mr. Potato Head was invented in 1949 and marketed by Hasbro in 1952. It's the first toy ever advertised on television.

Notes:

Viscum album
Mistletoe, Herbe de la Croix

Description: The Genus *Viscum* comprises about thirty Species known throughout the world. Mistletoe is an evergreen parasitic plant, growing on the branches of almost any deciduous tree, preferring those with soft bark. The stem is yellowish, with yellowish-green, leathery leaves. Inconspicuous white flowers are arranged in threes, opening in May. The familiar white berries ripen in December.

Cultivation: Completed naturally through the agency of birds. Once in contact with a tree, the sticky berry will send out a thread-like root which pierces the tree bark and feeds *off the tree*. One may rub fresh berries on the underside of a branch or make a few clefts in the branch for this purpose.

Parts Used: Twigs.

Poison: All parts of the plant. Toxicity Level II.

Side Effects: Berries are emetic and purgative. Overdose may lead to strong thirst, painful defecation with bloody feces, convulsion and gastrointestinal disorders. However, symptoms will subside and are rarely fatal. Mistletoe *can* absorb toxic constituents of its host tree.

Medicinal Uses: Extracts are used today under proper supervision for treatment of high blood pressure, poor circulation, as a sedative and in support of cancer treatments. It was used until recently to cure the "falling sickness" – epilepsy.

Saxons would pound the whole plant with roses and use as a plaster on the face for headaches; mix it with wine as a wash for sore eyes; or drink the same wine mixture from the rind of a pomegranate for kidney pain. Older writers recommended Mistletoe for sterility. (This, too, probably comes from the Druids who thought Mistletoe would cure barrenness – probably due to the fact that the berries' juice looks very much like semen.)

Magical Uses: The early Celts and Druids considered Mistletoe a sacred plant and specific rites were used to gather it. It was held to protect its possessor from evil. Probably due to the fact that it grows seemingly without any nourishment, it is useful in fertility spells; indeed, Mistletoe is part of the fertility rites of the Norse. It's used frequently in love spells (See **Interesting Tidbits** below) and to overcome obstacles.

Even today in Sweden, epileptics carry a knife with a handle made of Mistletoe growing from Oak to ward off attacks.

Interesting Tidbits: A Norse myth tells us that Baldur's mother had all creation swear not to harm her son but forgot to include Mistletoe in the oath. Loki tricked Baldur's blind brother into casting a Mistletoe wand at Baldur, who died from the shot. He was restored to life at the request of the other gods and goddesses. Mistletoe was given into the keeping of the goddess of Love and it was ordained that all who passed under it should be given a kiss to show that Mistletoe was now an emblem of love, not hate.

The common name, Herbe de la Croix, comes to us from Brittany where legend says the Cross was made from Mistletoe wood.

The Druids called it "all heal" and it is still known by this name in parts of Wales and Scotland.

Because of Mistletoe's association with the Druids, it was deemed a "pagan plant" and its use as Christmas decoration in churches was banned, even into the 20th century.

Pollen of Mistletoe was found in the stomach contents of Lindow Man, a well-preserved corpse found in a peat bog in Cheshire, England. He was thought to have lived the twenty-five or so years of his life between approximately 2 BCE and 119 CE.

Notes:

.SECTION THREE

In The Garden

All of the plants in this section may be found in cultivated gardens all over the world. You can even buy seeds and starter plants at the local landscape supply house. They may be pretty but some of them are pretty deadly.

Alkanna tinctoria
Alkanna, Alkanet, Anchusa, Dyers Bugloss

Description: A native of Central and Southern Europe and cultivated worldwide as an ornamental, Alkanna is a perennial, growing to approximately eight inches high by a foot wide. The leaves are oblong, the stem rising from a root much larger than one would think when just looking at the plant. The flowers are blue and usually appear in June.

Cultivation: Alkanna prefers a sandy or loamy well-drained soil in a partially shaded area such as woodland dappled shade. Seeds can be sown in a cold frame in the spring and planted outdoors when they become large enough to handle, or directly sown after the last frost. Propagation is also easy by cuttings taken in the late spring or root division in winter.

Parts Used: Root.

Poison: The root. Toxicity Level II.

Side Effects: The root contains pyrrolizidine alkaloids, which are mutagenic and carcinogenic. Substantial ingestion may cause gastrointestinal and central nervous system disturbance.

Medicinal Uses: No longer used internally, a decoction of the root in wine was once taken for back pains and illnesses such as smallpox, measles and leprosy. Its antibacterial, astringent and vulnerary properties make it good in an ointment for varicose veins, bed sores and itchy rashes. In 2005, Greek researchers found that an extract of the root showed antiradical activity, suggesting it has anti-aging properties.

Magical Uses: The root is burned alone or in combination as incense to attract prosperity and confer protection.

Interesting Tidbits: The root has been used for centuries as a dye. When extracted in oil, it yields a red coloring that once was used to color salves, stain wood in imitation of rosewood or mahogany, stain while marble to a flesh color, or to color fake port wine.

It is said that French ladies in the 16th century would use this dye as a temporary face color (perhaps as rouge).

Notes:

Anagallis arvensis
Scarlet Pimpernel

Description: Found along roadsides and in waste areas throughout the temperate regions of the world. It has creeping, square stems, no more than a foot in length with egg-shaped leaves arising directly off the stem. Single flowers appear from May to late August and are reddish, sometimes with a purple spot in the center.

Cultivation: An annual, cultivation is strictly by seed. Sow outdoors after the last frost, thinning to six inches apart. It prefers a sunny location and well-drained soil. It will readily re-seed itself after the initial planting. In many places, it is considered an invasive weed.

Parts Used: Aerial.

Poison: All parts of the plant but especially the root. Toxicity Level II.

Side Effects: High doses will produce gastrointestinal problems, trembling and kidney damage. It is also slightly narcotic. Experiments in the 1800's proved that high doses were fatal to dogs.

Medicinal Uses: Rarely used today but for many years a decoction or tincture was used to dispel melancholy and treat epilepsy. A strong infusion was given for feverish complaints; the tincture was also said to be effective in urinary tract issues. Pliny valued it in liver complaints. Its Genus name, *Anagallis* was given to it by Dioscorides and is derived from the Greek *Anagelao,* meaning 'to laugh', which one was said to do after being cured from liver disease.

Magical Uses: Used in protection spells, especially from mental attack. In some circles, the juice of the plant is used to consecrate the ritual knife, the boline. At one time, Christians said a prayer holding the flower to protect them from witches.

Interesting Tidbits: The flowers are extremely sensitive, closing at the first hint of rain and even on nice days, only open from morning to mid-afternoon. From this the common names, 'Poor Man's Weatherglass' and 'Shepherd's Barometer', were derived. The color is only on the top of the petal, making the flowers nearly disappear back into the stalk when closed.

In 1934 and again in 1982, the classic adventure novel, *The Scarlet Pimpernel* by Baroness Orczy was adapted into a movie. The flower is a symbol of both the hero's family (he wears a signet ring with the flower prominent) and of the hero himself (his pseudonym).

Notes:

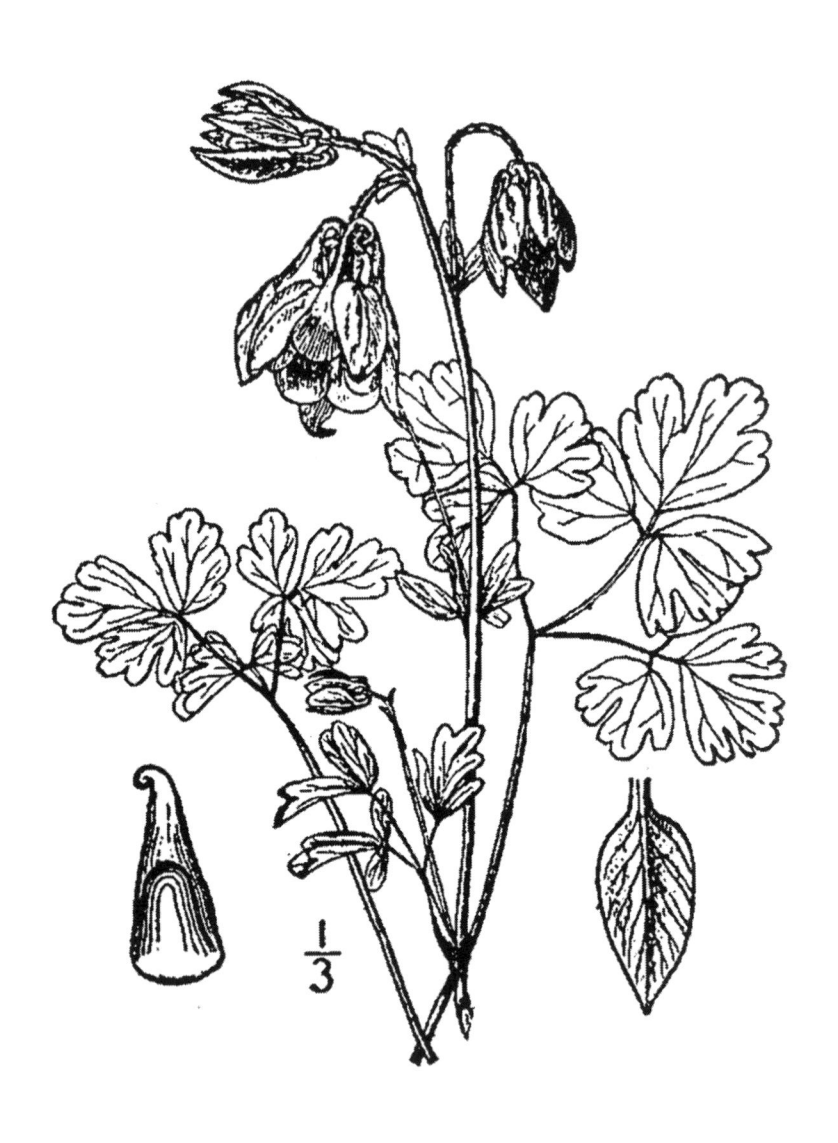

Aquilegia vulgaris

Aquilegia vulgaris
Columbine

Description: A native of Europe, it has become naturalized in the eastern United States. Columbine's stem is slightly hairy and grows from one to two feet high. The leaves, which are large at the base of the plant and get smaller the higher you go, are dark, bluish-green on top and grayish-green below. Nodding flowers appear in May and June and are usually blue or dull purple but sometimes white. They have five petals that contain backward-projecting spurs, which contain the nectar.

Cultivation: Columbine may be found wild in both woodlands and open fields, although it's more familiar as a perennial garden flower. While very adaptable, it prefers rich, moist soil in partial shade. Sow seeds directly in the garden after the danger of frost has passed. They should be left uncovered (or covered only with a net to deter birds) as they will germinate faster in sunlight. Thin seedlings to a foot apart. Those in colder climates should provide a good cover of mulch in the fall to protect the plants from freezing temperatures. They will self-seed but the production of seed shortens the life span of the plant, so plan on replacing or overseeding every 3-4 years.

Parts Used: All.

Poison: All parts of the plant but especially the seeds. Toxicity Level II.

Side Effects: High doses produce dizziness, pupil dilation, respiratory distress and unconsciousness. Fatalities in children have been reported after ingestion of the seeds.

Medicinal Uses: A decoction of the root is used to stop diarrhea; a wine tincture of the flowers will promote perspiration; a wine tincture of the seeds was once used to speed childbirth. A lotion of the leaves is used for sore mouths and throats and a lotion made from the fresh root will alleviate rheumatic pain.

Magical Uses: Rubbing the juice of fresh leaves on your body is said to confer courage in difficult situations. Rubbing the pulverized seeds between your hands will attract love.

Interesting Tidbits: The Genus name, *Aquilegia* is from the Latin *Aquila*, an eagle. It was thought the flower spurs resembled an eagle's talons. The common name, Columbine, is also avian in nature: *Columba* is Latin for "dove", from the flower's resemblance to those birds in flight. An even older name, *Culverwort,* is Saxon: *culfre* means "pigeon" and *wort* is Saxon for "plant".

According to Culpeper, "The Spaniards used to eat a piece of the root thereof in a morning fasting many days together, to help them when troubled with stone."

Columbine is one of the badges of the House of Lancaster and also the House of Derby.

The Rocky Mountain Columbine (*Aquilegia caerulea*) was adopted as the State Flower of Colorado in 1899 and was protected by Colorado law in 1925. It is illegal to uproot this plant on public land and collection of the flowers and buds is limited to 25 per day.

Notes:

Asclepias tuberosa
Milkweed, Butterfly Weed, Pleurisy Root

Description: One of approximately 100 members of the *Asclepias* Genus. *A. tuberosa* is native to eastern North America. It is perennial, growing up to three feet high with spirally-arranged, lance-like leaves around the hairy stem. Broad clusters of orange or yellow flowers appear early summer to early fall. The seed capsules follow the flowers and will split open when ripe, releasing seeds with silky hairs. It is sometimes mistaken for its cousin, *A. lanceolata*, but can easily be differentiated by the larger number of flowers and nearly no latex in the stem.

Cultivation: Grows easily from seed in well-drained sandy soils. Plant in spring after the danger of frost has passed in full sun to partial shade. It is also easily cultivated from root cuttings. The plant will take two to three years to fully mature and produce flowers but once established, will become thicker with each successive year. Note: susceptible to aphids.

Parts Used: Root, rhizome.

Poison: All parts of the plant. Toxicity Level II.

Side Effects: Overdose symptoms are those experienced with any cardiac glycoside poisoning: nausea, excessive salivation, gastrointestinal disturbance, arrhythmia, hypertension, coma, cardiac arrest.

Medicinal Uses: A traditional treatment for pleurisy, bronchitis and other respiratory infections, the root has also been used by Native Americans for treatment of epilepsy, kidney and stomach troubles, and syphilis.

Magical Uses: An infusion of the root may be used as a body wash to confer strength in sporting contests or to dampen one's running shoes for speed.

Interesting Tidbits: The plant fibers are used for cordage and to make belts. The latex is used by Native Americans as candy and chewing gum (although other Species of *Asclepias* will yield more latex than *A. tuberosa*).

Notes:

Brugmansia spp.
Angel's Trumpet, Tree Datura

Description: There are 14 recognized Species in this Genus, although many hybrids may be found. Native to tropical regions of South America, it's a perennial shrub or small tree with large leaves that may be covered with hairs, depending on the Species. The flowers are large and pendulous, resembling a trumpet. Flowers are quite fragrant (especially in the evenings) and may be almost any color. *Brugmansia* are frequently confused with *Datura* (the difference in Species wasn't settled until 1973) but where *Brugmansia* flowers are pendulous, those of *Datura* Species are upright.

Cultivation: Widely grown as an ornamental tree in tropical regions and as a container plant worldwide, they prefer moist, well-drained soil and sun to partial shade. If you have a friend with a *Brugmansia* already established, take a cutting from the end of a branch during summer and root it. Those experiencing mild winters may see the plant die back in late fall but if the roots are well mulched, it will reappear in the spring. Flowers appear in mid- to late spring and with proper care, will bloom almost until fall.

Parts Used: Leaves.

Poison: All parts of the plant. Toxicity Level I.

Side Effects: As with any member of the Solanaceae family, it contains many alkaloids that, in small doses, produce a sedative effect. Higher doses lead to hallucinations, confusion, insomnia, death from respiratory arrest. Mydriasis (pupil dilation) may last as long as six days. Many hospitalizations and some fatalities of teenagers have been reported (especially in Florida and California) after ingestion of a tea made from Angel's Trumpet.

Medicinal Uses: Many of the alkaloids found in *Brugmansia* are now synthesized and used by the medical community for their anti-asthmatic, narcotic and anesthetic qualities. Some native peoples of South America still use it externally to treat arthritis, rheumatism, headaches, and infections via tincture, poultice or ointment. In extreme cases, highly diluted preparations are used as a decongestant, vermifuge, sedative, and to induce vomiting.

Magical Uses: As with *Datura*, it is smoked or drunk as a tea to induce visions and by some native peoples, in initiation rites, healing ceremonies and shamanic journeying.

Interesting Tidbits: It is said that the hallucinogenic effects of *Brugmansia* are terrifying, rather than pleasurable. *Psychiatry and Clinical Neuroscience* reported in 2006 that a young man amputated his own penis and tongue after drinking only one cup of tea.

B. arborea is regarded as one of the most ancient healing herbs by people indigenous to the Andes of Peru and Ecuador and was thought to be employed as a narcotic and anesthetic in ritual or medicinal operations – including trepanning.

Tribes of the Sibundoy region of Colombia mix *Brugmansia* into dog food as a part of a hunting magic ritual. It's thought the dogs participate in the ritual and are then able to see their prey more easily.

Notes:

Buxus sempervirens
Box

Description: A native of the Mediterranean area, today it is cultivated worldwide as an ornamental and hedge plant. Familiar to most as a shrub, if left alone it will grow to a small tree no more than 20 feet high with rough, grayish bark and densely leafy branches. The leaves are small, smooth and dark green. Flowers are in clusters with a single female flower and many male ones. The fruit is a green capsule which will explode and shoot the seed out.

Cultivation: Box grows best from a cutting, which is best taken while pruning, in either May or August (in northern climates). It is tolerant of most any soil, as long as it has good drainage and isn't allowed to completely dry out. Prefers partial sun but will do well in full shade, making it an ideal understory plant. This is a rare plant in that if an older shrub has been neglected, it will respond well to a hard pruning (down to approximately a foot from the ground).

Parts Used: Leaves, bark, wood.

Poison: The aerial portions of the plant. Toxicity Level I.

Side Effects: Ingestion causes irritation of the gastrointestinal tract, diarrhea, vomiting, dizziness, hypotension, seizures and finally death by paralysis (respiratory arrest).

Medicinal Uses: No longer in use medicinally, it was once used to treat rheumatism and venereal disease. The tincture was once considered a remedy for leprosy and the essential oil was used to treat hemorrhoids. Not only the oil but honey produced by bees feeding on Box was taken to treat epilepsy. Powdered leaves were taken as a vermifuge.

Magical Uses: A Box planted by the house is said to ward off lightning and planted around a field, will protect the crops. Carrying a sprig of Box on a journey will bring good luck. Leaves placed in the shoes of a pregnant woman will protect her during childbirth. In Germany and Flanders, spoon and knife handles made from Boxwood will remove lecherous desires. In parts of Belgium, hanging a sprig of Box on the chimney is considered a remedy for sore throats.

Interesting Tidbits: Hildegard von Bingen (1098-1179) described Box as having the power to combat baldness.

The leaves and sawdust were boiled in lye and used to dye the hair an auburn color; as late as the early 1900's, the powdered leaves were given to horses to improve their coats. The wood is very durable, insect-resistant and difficult to split. It has been used since Antiquity as a veneer and in the production of musical instruments (flutes and clarinets), pipe bowls, combs and wood engravings. Flutes made of Box were played by the 1st century CE Tuscans during their religious rituals.

In Greek Antiquity, Box was dedicated to Hades, Aphrodite/Venus and Cybele.

Notes:

Chrysanthemum vulgare (syn. Tanacetum vulgare)
Tansy

Description: Common to the dry and waste places of Europe and Asia, it is now cultivated in gardens worldwide. An erect perennial growing to about 3 feet high, it has jagged, dark green leaves. Conspicuous, bright yellow flowers appear in flat clusters in late summer. The flowers are button-like and lack ray florets. Its odor is somewhat disagreeable, bearing a resemblance to camphor.

Cultivation: Although it will grow from seed, it is most easily cultivated by taking a slip or dividing the roots, either in spring or fall. It will thrive in most any soil with full sun and has moderate water requirements.

Parts Used: Aerial.

Poison: All parts but especially the flowers. Toxicity Level II.

Side Effects: The plant is toxic due to the thujone in the essential oil. Large doses (or ingestion over long periods of time) may cause abortion, vomiting, gastrointestinal problems, convulsions, arrhythmia, kidney and liver damage, coma and death.

Medicinal Uses: As noted above, Tansy is used to cause abortions. In the hands of a professional, it is used to treat amenorrhea, migraine, liver complaints, loss of appetite, scabies and worms.

Magical Uses: Alone or in combination with other herbs, Tansy may be used to maintain health or confer longevity.

Interesting Tidbits: The name, Tansy, may be derived from the Greek *Athanaton* (immortal). It's thought this may be because Tansy flowers last for a long time compared to other plants or because the Ancient Greeks used it to preserve dead bodies. It was said Tansy was given to Ganymede to make him immortal.

Tansy was once one of the "Strewing Herbs", perhaps because it was thought to keep flies away.

During Easter time, clergy took on their congregation in a game of handball. Tansy cakes were the reward of the victors.

The Ojibwa tribe of North America use the herb in a hunting incense used to attract deer.

Notes:

Cyclamen spp.
Cyclamen

Description: The Genus has 19 Species, native to Europe and the Mediterranean area but is well-known as a container plant throughout the world. This perennial grows low to the ground and has simple, heart-shaped leaves that are leathery and dark green with pale green or whitish lines. White, pink or purple flowers appear on naked stems during summer. These stems roll up when the seeds are produced so the seeds mature under the protection of the leaves.

Cultivation: Easily acquired as a potted plant at most landscape supply stores, seeds are available from some sources. Cyclamen isn't picky about its soil but will grow best in dirt that is slightly alkaline, well drained and in partial shade. Some Species are frost-hardy, others are not so you'll need to check. It is very susceptible to fungus and other diseases as well as a variety of insects.

Parts Used: The root.

Poison: All parts of the plant but especially the tuber. Toxicity Level II.

Side Effects: The plant sap may cause skin irritation. Ingestion may produce severe stomach pain, nausea, vomiting, diarrhea, circulatory problems, convulsions and respiratory arrest.

Medicinal Uses: Cyclamen is a drastic purgative. A decoction of the dried root has been used in cases of colds, flu, flatulence, and intestinal worms. Fresh tubers are pounded and applied to a festering sore.

Magical Uses: The root, pounded and baked into little cakes will cause the eater to fall in love with the baker.

Interesting Tidbits: Pliny the Elder reports that *Cyclamen* was used as an arrowhead poison and it has been used as a fish poison.

Notes:

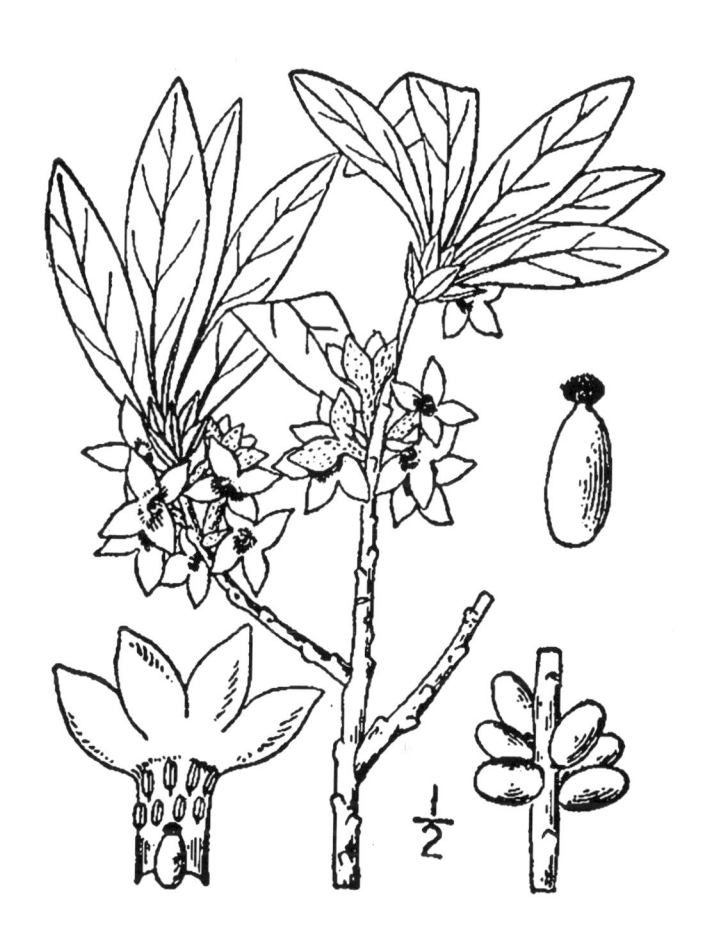

Daphne mezereum

Daphne spp.

Daphne, others depending on Species

Description: There are 50 Species in this Genus; Eurasian in origin but cultivated all over the world for their showy and fragrant flowers. They are generally perennial, deciduous shrubs, growing up to 5 feet tall with tough, gray-brown bark and smooth, oval, pale green leaves. The white, pink or purple flowers generally emerge before the leaves from February to April. Red or yellow berries follow.

Cultivation: Depending on the Species, moist, loamy soil in a location that gets partial sun. For best results, purchase a seedling from a trusted source and follow their instructions.

Parts Used: Bark of root and stem; berries.

Poison: All parts of the plant. Toxicity Level I. The berries are attractive but only 2-3 berries for a child or 10-12 for an adult may be fatal.

Side Effects: Ingestion produces a strong burning sensation in the mouth and throat, excessive salivation, swallowing difficulties, bloody vomiting and/or diarrhea, spasms, paralysis, tachycardia, circulatory collapse leading to death. Even external exposure to the fresh plant may evoke skin inflammation and necrotic blisters.

Medicinal Uses: Rarely used today in a medicinal context, although the berries have been used as a purgative, emetic and in some cancer treatments. Roots of *D. laureola* were once applied and/or chewed to alleviate a toothache, or swallowed as an abortifacient. The seeds of *D. mezereum* have been swallowed like pills to cure piles. The Cherokee use the root bark of *D. mezereum* for venereal disease pains. In the 19th century, *D. mezereum* was an ingredient in the official medicinal compound Sarsaparilla and it had a one-time reputation as a remedy in the secondary stages of venereal disease.

Magical Uses: None known.

Interesting Tidbits Beggars are known to inflict skin wounds on their intended targets with extracts of *D. mezereum* to "induce compassion".

D. cneorum is used as a fish poison.

The root bark is occasionally used for writing quills.

Culpeper called *D. mezereum* "Widdow-wail".

Notes:

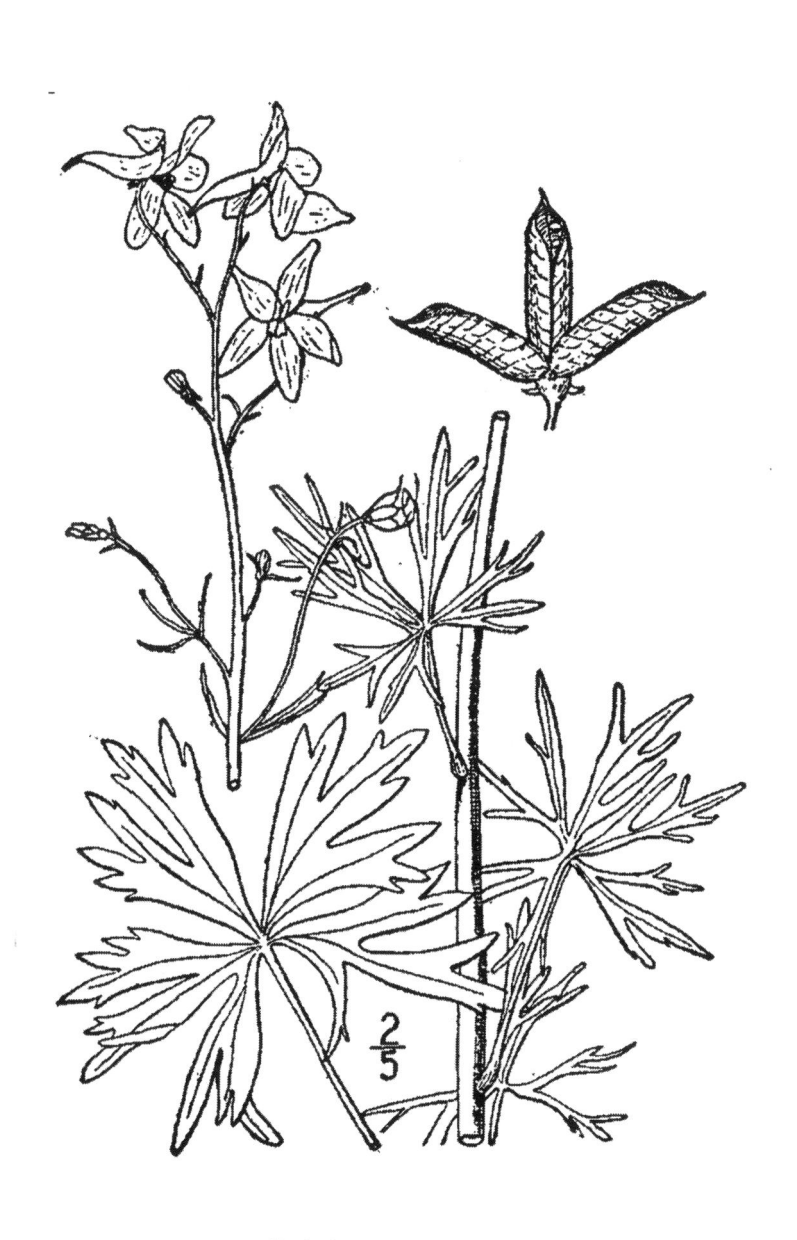

Delphinium tricorne

Delphinium spp.

Delphinium, Larkspur, Lark's Heel

Description: More than 300 Species comprise this Genus. Larkspur is generally an annual with erect stems, a foot or more high. The leaves are smooth or toothed, depending on the Species. Purple, blue or white flowers grow all the way up the stem and appear in late spring through the summer.

Cultivation: Larkspur doesn't care whether the soil is rich, as long as it is well-drained. Prefers full sun but will tolerate light shade. Although an annual, it readily reseeds itself and may become invasive. Delphinium will bloom more profusely if it is dead-headed.

Parts Used: Seed.

Poison: All parts of the plant but especially the seed. Toxicity Level I.

Side Effects: Similar to aconite: nausea, cardiac arrhythmia, inflammation of the gastrointestinal tract, paralysis. Death may occur from respiratory and cardiac arrest.

Medicinal Uses: Not used today but in the past, a tincture was used in cases of spasmodic asthma and the juice of the leaves was used to alleviate piles. A tincture may be used as an insecticide, particularly for lice and nits.

Magical Uses: An amulet of the flowers worn around the neck is said to preserve one's eyesight. Grown near the house, it's said to protect from lightning strikes. The women of the Thompson tribe of North America use the plant as a charm to "help them obtain and hold the affection of men".

Interesting Tidbits: The juice of the petals of *D. consolida* mixed with alum yields a blue ink. Other Species are also used as a dye by some Native American tribes.

The effects of Delphinium were known in Pliny's time: he called it "Paralysis".

Some Native American tribes were aware of the narcotic effects of Larkspur and used it to daze opponents in gambling games.

The Genus name comes from the Greek *delphis* – a reference to the flower's resemblance to a bottle-nose dolphin.

Notes:

Dictamnus albus
Dittany, False Dittany, Burning Bush

Description: This is *not* Dittany of Crete – that is *Origanum dictamnus*. There is only one Species in this Genus but many cultivars. A perennial native to southern Europe, northern Africa and parts of Asia, it is now found in gardens in warmer climates. The plant grows up to 5 feet tall (usually 2-3 feet) with erect stems and leaves that resemble those of an Ash tree. The flowers vary in color from white to pale purple to blue to red and may even be striped. Flowers appear late spring well into the fall, depending on the cultivar.

Cultivation: Prefers moist but not necessarily rich soil, a sheltered location and a warm but not hot climate. May sometimes be found wild in woodlands. Sow outside in the fall or cold-stratify the seeds before planting in the spring. Requires only moderate watering.

Parts Used: Aerial.

Poison: The aerial portions of the plant and the essential oil. Toxicity Level II.

Side Effects: The aerial part of the plant is a skin irritant, especially the sap-like substance that covers it in the summer months. Contact dermatitis has been reported, as has photodermatitis when exposed to sunlight.

Medicinal Uses: Not in use today but the powdered root was once used in malignant and pestilential fevers, and epilepsy. An infusion of the aerial portion of the plant was used to treat gravel (kidney stones). Dioscorides used it as an abortifacient. It is known to have emmenagogue properties but its use is generally obsolete.

Magical Uses: None known

Interesting Tidbits: The plant exudes a sap-like substance that covers not only the stem but the leaves and flowers as well. This sap is *flammable* and may be easily ignited with a match. There have also been reports of the plant spontaneously combusting in the hot afternoon sun. The lemon-like essential oil is so strong that the daughter of Carl Linnaeus was able to light the air above a plant.

Notes:

Hedera helix
Common Ivy, English Ivy

Description: A well-known evergreen climber with glossy leaves. It climbs by means of little fibers extending from the roots that cling to whatever it's climbing and eventually form new roots. These roots, if adhering to soil or another living plant, will extract nourishment from its host. It does produce small, greenish-yellow flowers in late fall but only after it has climbed *above* its host. Black or deep purple berries appear the spring following flowering.

Cultivation: Should you find a plant that has produced berries and can rescue those berries from the birds, there are two to five seeds inside each one. Most Ivy is rooted from cuttings off a parent plant, which is then transplanted outdoors in the spring. It will grow in most any soil, in shady to partly-shady spots.

Parts Used: Leaves and berries.

Poison: All parts of the plant. Toxicity Level: II.

Side Effects: The berries are very bitter and will discourage children from eating them. 2-3 berries will cause toxic symptoms in a child, although fatalities are rare. Symptoms include nausea, vomiting, headache, dizziness, delirium, and respiratory arrest. Contact dermatitis has been reported by gardeners pruning and training the vines.

Medicinal Uses: Rarely used today, but an infusion of the dried leaves is said to be helpful in cases of catarrh or bronchitis, and to counteract the effects of alcohol. Extracts of ivy wood are emollient and are added to soothing skin preparations: an old English remedy for sunburn was to boil fresh twigs in butter and smear on the affected part and this is still done today in the Highlands of Scotland. Culpeper said that the berries were used to "prevent and heal the plague". (What doesn't kill you makes you stronger?)

Magical Uses: Ivy is worn or carried for good luck. An ivy wreath was presented to a newlywed couple by Greek priests as an emblem of fidelity. It is said that Ivy guards against negativity, which perhaps is the reason behind allowing it to grow on the sides of houses. It's also said that Dionysus' stepmother, Hera, wanted to destroy him and to prevent her from doing so, his nursemaids screened his crib with Ivy leaves.

Interesting Tidbits: Ivy ale was brewed at Oxford University in medieval times; English taverns would display an Ivy bush above their doors to indicate excellent liquor within.

Ivy can grow to a great age and there have been ivy trunks a foot or more in diameter. Although the wood is soft, it is used by wood turners in some parts of southern Europe.

The custom of decorating with Ivy at Christmas was forbidden by one of the early Councils of the Church due to its pagan associations. It seems that edict was ignored, as the custom still remains.

Notes:

Ilex aquifolium
Holly, English Holly

Description: Approximately 400 Species comprise the Genus *Ilex*, and they are found throughout the world. *I. aquifolium* is a native of central and southern Europe but has been naturalized in many parts of the world. Holly is a tree that can reach 40 feet but is usually found as a 6-7 foot shrub. The bark is usually light gray but may be touched with red. The leaves are thick and leathery, and edged with prickles. Although considered an evergreen, it is deciduous: the leaves will occasionally drop individually after several years. It produces whitish flowers in May but female and male flowers are on different plants. The familiar red berries appear after flowering.

Cultivation: Holly will grow in almost any soil but prefers something light with good drainage. The berries contain several seeds which, when planted, will germinate during the second year. It is greedy and will exhaust the surrounding soil, sometimes injuring neighboring trees. Once established, it will grow quickly as long as it is not overwatered.

Parts Used: Leaves and berries.

Poison: All parts of the plant but especially the berries. Toxicity Level I.

Side Effects: 20-30 berries are lethal for most humans and toxic symptoms are produced when ingesting only 5 berries. Sleepiness, vomiting, diarrhea, cardiac arrhythmia, paralysis, kidney damage and even death have been reported.

Medicinal Uses An infusion of the leaves is used to treat arthritis, fever and jaundice. This must be done under proper supervision due to the low therapeutic margin. A fomentation of the bark and leaves was once used to treat broken bones.

Magical Uses: A Holly is planted near the house to provide a guard. According to Pliny, it "repels poison, defends from lightning and keeps off witchcrafts". Carrying a few berries, especially by men, will promote good luck.

Interesting Tidbits: Many indigenous tribes believe a Holly should never be cut down – to do so will bring death to the cutter.

If one throws a piece of Holly wood at an animal, it will compel the animal to return and lie down.

Some Native American tribes make "black drink" from *I. cassine* or *I. vomitoria* due to their stimulating properties. This drink, together with tobacco, induces bravery for going into battle. Alone, the drink is taken to clear out the system and produce ceremonial purity.

The Species *I. paraguariensis* is the source of maté tea.

Notes:

Kalanchoe lanceolata
Kalanchoe

Description: One of approximately 125 Species, most Kalanchoes are natives of the tropics, especially Africa and Madagascar. Most are shrubs, perennial and herbaceous (drop their leaves in winter) but a few are annual or biennial. They generally grow less than 3 feet tall with succulent, bright green leaves. Countless flowers may be yellow, orange, pink or purplish.

Cultivation: Especially in the colder areas of the world, Kalanchoe can be found in stores during the holiday season. (I can remember seeing it marketed as a "Christmas Plant".) If you have an existing plant, cultivation is easy. Cut a healthy leaf off with a sharp knife and strip the leaf along one side to expose the sap. Place the cut portion into moistened sand far enough in so the leaf stands on its own. In about a month, you'll see a new plant or two emerging from the base of the leaf. Gently dig the new plants from the sand (the roots are very fragile) and transplant into their own pot, ensuring the soil is well-drained (at least half sand or perlite). Full-to-partial sun is recommended.

Unless you live in a tropical climate, Kalanchoes must be treated as treasured houseplants. In a tropical climate, they make beautiful additions to rock or succulent gardens.

Parts Used: Leaves, leaf juice.

Poison: The aerial portions of the plant. Toxicity Level II.

Side Effects: Although Kalanchoe contains cardiac glycosides, the symptoms are different than most: exhaustion, paralysis (especially of the head and neck), convulsions, respiratory paralysis and eventually, death. There have been reports of livestock eating Kalanchoe and laying on their sides, totally paralyzed but conscious for several weeks before succumbing.

Medicinal Uses: Various Species of Kalanchoe are used by indigenous peoples to treat: infected wounds, inflammation, hypertension, diarrhea, mental illness, cancer, migraines, headaches, heartburn, urinary tract infection, toothaches, burns, and insect bites; as a cough suppressant, to promote menstruation and assist in childbirth. Some healers use it to treat antibiotic-resistant bacterial infections. The most common use is as a poultice or in an ointment externally, as an infusion of the leaves, ingestion of the leaf juice or adding the young leaves to salads.

Magical Uses: None known.

Interesting Tidbits: In the Language of Flowers, Kalanchoe means "Endurance", "Popularity" or "Lasting Affection".

The Chinese use Kalanchoe extensively as decoration during their New Year. Their name for it translates as "Thousand and Millions of Red and Purple".

Notes :

Narcissus spp.

Daffodil, Narcissus, Jonquil

Description: This highly popular garden flower has approximately 27 Species and many, many cultivars. The bulb puts up dark green, spear-like leaves with a single flower stalk. Flowers, which appear in spring, are showy and usually some shade of yellow, although some cultivars will produce white flowers.

Cultivation: Narcissus are very adaptable and will grow in nearly any climate. Plant bulbs in the fall for showy spring flowers. Some bulbs produce baby bulbs right next to them. These can be divided after flowering and planted on their own; it may take from two to seven years (depending on Species) before they flower. Seeds may also be collected and planted, although the seeds may not produce true to the parent. As a showy flower, Narcissus requires at least partial sun. While not subject to a lot of disease, do not overwater and rot the bulb.

Parts Used: Bulb, flower, leaves.

Poison: All parts but especially the bulb. Toxicity Level I.

Side Effects: The bulbs sometimes resemble an onion and may be taken for such by children. Symptoms include excessive salivation, vomiting and diarrhea, leading to paralysis, liver damage and possibly death. Contact dermatitis may be experienced when handling the bulbs with bare hands – it's even called "daffodil itch".

Medicinal Uses: Due to the toxic nature, Narcissus is no longer used in a medicinal sense. A drug synthesized from the daffodil has been studied for treating Alzheimer's disease with some success in helping delay or prevent memory loss. Other chemical extracts are being studied for possible anti-cancer activity. Culpeper once used the bulbs of *white* Narcissus as a purgative, and mixed ground bulbs with barley and honey for wounds and sprains. The bruised leaves were once used in the British Isles as a cure for erysipelas – a reddening of the skin which was associated with ergot poisoning.

Magical Uses: Fresh flowers kept in the bedroom will promote fertility; or place them on your altar for love spells.

The Arabians used the blooms as an aphrodisiac. *However*, it is said that the scent of *N. poetica* will cause headaches and vomiting if the blooms are kept in a closed room.

Interesting Tidbits: While most think the Genus name came from the vain Greek youth, it is actually from the Greek word, *narkao*, because of its narcotic properties.

Greek and Roman women used a paste of honey and powdered Narcissus bulbs to whiten their skin; Porta said that the roots steeped in wine and then poured on a shaved scalp would cause the growing hair to curl.

In parts of England, the Daffodil was banned from the house by poultry-keepers. They said the eggs wouldn't hatch.

Notes:

Prunus laurocerasus
Cherry Laurel, Cherry Bay

Description: Native to Asia Minor but cultivated all over the northern hemisphere, the Cherry Laurel is a small evergreen shrub or tree, reaching up to twenty feet in height and popular as a hedge. The leaves are simple, glossy and bright green and often mistaken for Bay leaves (*Laurus nobilis*). The small, white flowers grow on erect racemes, giving way to black berries that ripen in the fall and very much resemble black cherries.

Cultivation: Plant the seeds in well-drained soil in either sun or shade. They require very little attention and are drought-resistant, but are susceptible to root rot if overwatered. Prune in spring or fall, depending on whether you want a hedge or an individual tree.

Parts Used: Fresh leaves.

Poison: All parts, especially the seeds, except the ripe fruit. Toxicity Level II. The fruit is edible but somewhat bland compared to its relatives.

Side Effects: Human poisoning is rare but symptoms are typical for any cyanide poisoning: irritation, flushing, scratchy throat and in severe cases, respiratory and cardiac arrest.

Medicinal Uses: No longer currently used in a medicinal sense but Cherry Laurel water was once used as a respiratory stimulant in cases of asthma or coughs. It is also narcotic and its use for suicide and murder is well-known. Like most members of the *Prunus* genus, the leaves and pips contain cyanide.

Magical Uses: None known.

Interesting Tidbits: Cherry Laurel Water was passed off as Kirsch in Paris in the 1800's; fresh leaves are still occasionally used to flavor milk and cream.

The leaves have no odor unless crushed, when they smell similar to bitter almonds. The vapor arising from the plant (probably when an animal brushes up against it) is toxic to insects.

Notes:

Rheum rhaponticum
Garden Rhubarb

Description: The Genus *Rheum* comprises approximately 30 Species native to Europe and Asia; the parent Species has been traced back to China and Tibet. Several are used in herbal medicine. All are perennial herbs with thick stems below ground and large leaves at the top of bright red petioles (stalks). Small flowers appear in tall clusters; color is dependent on Species.

Cultivation: Although Rhubarb will grow from seed, it may be easier to obtain an established plant from the nursery. Sow seeds in the open after the danger of frost has passed, thinning to about a foot apart when at least two leaves have appeared. Once matured, move your plants to their final bed, allowing four feet around each. Rhubarb prefers rich soil (manure is an excellent mulch for this plant) and has moderate watering requirements.

Parts Used: Root and rhizome.

Poison: All parts of the plant, especially the leaves. Toxicity Level III.

Side Effects: Ingestion of a few pieces of pie, or even a jar of jam won't bother most people but eating *large* amounts of Rhubarb may produce irregular pulse, hypotension, collapse, coma and death by paralysis or irreparable harm to the kidneys. People with kidney disease are especially vulnerable and children may develop kidney problems after eating even a small amount.

Medicinal Uses: *R. officinale* and *R. palmatum* are the two Species most frequently used in a medicinal context. Both the root and seed of *R. rhaponticum* have been used in the past as an appetite stimulant and like its cousins, to treat either diarrhea or constipation (small doses for the former, larger for the latter).

Magical Uses: A piece of the root worn or carried will ensure the health of one's stomach. It is said that serving a piece of pie to your significant other will ensure his/her fidelity.

Interesting Tidbits: Infusing the root in water and adding a pinch of Cream of Tartar will produce a red dye. *Rheum* is one of the few Genera of plants that will change the color of urine, in this case, to red or bright yellow.

Notes:

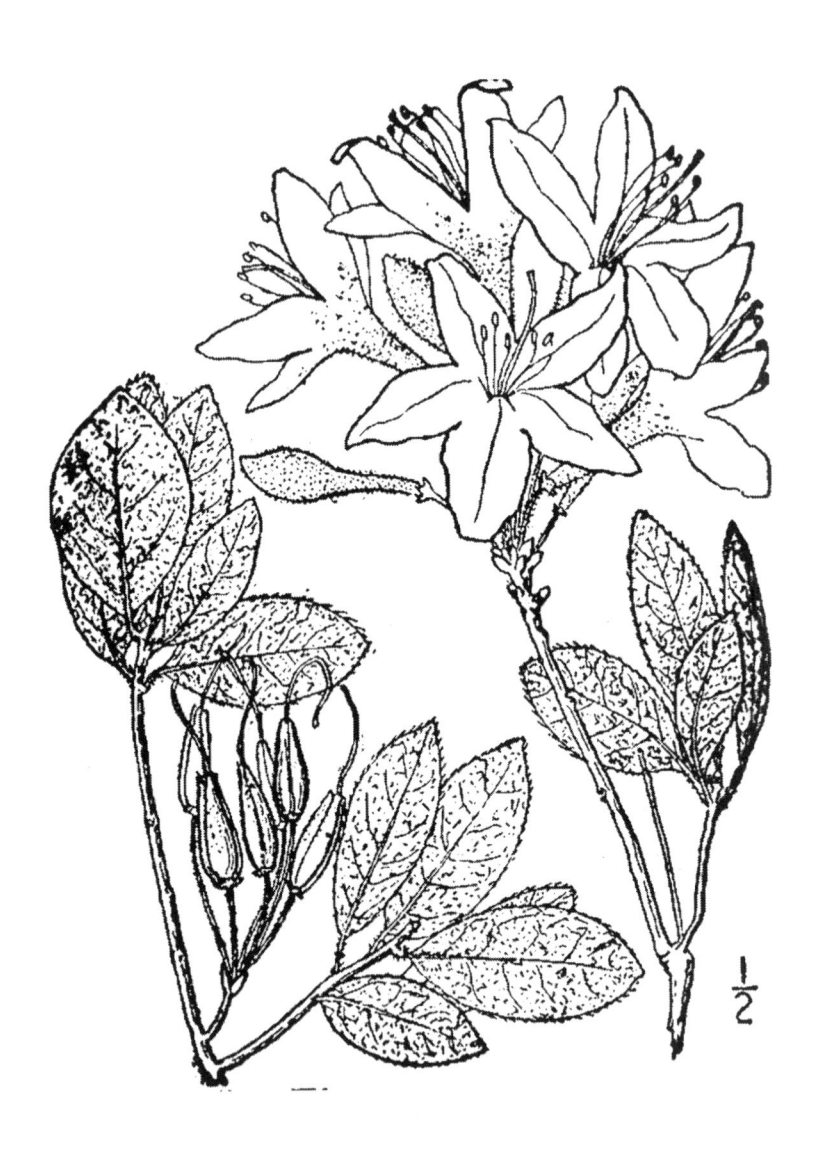

Rhododendron canescens

Rhododendron spp.
Rhododendron, Azalea

Description: The Rhododendron Genus comprises more than 850 Species, many of which are cultivated as ornamental plants. They are native to the Iberian Peninsula but are now naturalized in all parts of the world. Most Species are small, evergreen shrubs but some may be deciduous and/or reach five feet or more in height and width. Large, showy flowers appear in the spring. Some Species will flower until the fall if deadheaded with regularity.

Cultivation: May be propagated from seed or cuttings. Most Species will thrive in almost any environment but they all like moist soil. Follow instructions for the Species you are planting for best results.

Parts Used: Leaves.

Poison: All parts of the plant. Toxicity Level I.

Side Effects: An initial burning sensation in the mouth gives way to excessive salivation, difficulty in swallowing, intoxication, irregular pulse, arrhythmia, arterial hypotension, and death from respiratory arrest. Contact dermatitis may be experienced when picking flowers.

Medicinal Uses: Extracts of *R. tomentosum* are made into "Marsh Tea", which is then used in a syrup for treatment of pertussis (whooping cough). This tea is also used in anti-rheumatic, emetic, diuretic and diaphoretic medicines. Native Americans use the burned and powdered wood in a salve for swellings, Other Species are used by natives in northern Asia and North America for treating rheumatism and gout.

While not exactly medicinal, the leaves are traditionally used to ward off moths and bedbugs.

Magical Uses: The Karok use *R. macrophyllum* in a luck-getting ceremony of the sweat house. Asian Shamans inhaled the smoke from burning leaves as an intoxicant, allowing them to "reach the other side".

The women of the Thompson tribe use Rhododendron as a scent. They also contract a lot of contact dermatitis while gathering the flowers.

Interesting Tidbits: Honey made by bees feasting on Rhododendron flowers is toxic. In 401 BCE, Xenophon decided that his large army needed a rest and camped in a beautiful place surrounded by Rhododendrons in Colchis, near the Black Sea. The only problem they encountered (they thought) was the numbers of swarming bees. The soldiers found the hives and raided them for the honey inside. Shortly after consuming the honey, the soldiers "succumbed to a strange affliction" and began to act intoxicated, staggering and collapsing by the thousands. Most were totally incapacitated; some died. Those that did recover found they couldn't stand for three or four days.

Nearly four centuries later, Pompey camped with his army in the same area with worse consequences. Everyone died. (Pompey apparently didn't read Xenophon's history.) Accounts of people getting sick and/or going crazy for a bit after eating honey harvested from Rhododendron-covered woods persist to this day.

Today, the honey made from Rhododendrons is known as deli bal (mad honey) in Turkey and the northern Caucasus (miel fou in the West) – and sold commercially. Folks put a little into milk for a pick-me-up or a dollop of it in their alcoholic beverage to give it a little kick.

The Vikings (and later, Germans) used the leaves of Rhododendron to increase the potency of their beer; this practice was banned in 1723 by the Duke of Hanover.

Notes:

Ruta graveolens
Rue

Description: Seven Species comprise this Genus, native to Europe, North Africa and western Asia, although it is now cultivated in gardens around the world. It is a small, evergreen shrub growing about three feet high with branched, pale green stems and somewhat fleshy leaves. Small, yellow flowers appear in clusters during the summer.

Cultivation: Rue is easily cultivated from cuttings taken in the spring, or by seeds planted (also in spring) with a light covering of soil. It seems to be happiest in poor, dry soil in a shady location.

Parts Used: Aerial.

Poison: All parts of the plant. Toxicity Level II.

Side Effects: Most people will suffer from an itchy, burning dermatitis if they handle the plant. Ingestion causes swelling of the tongue, excess salivation, severe gastrointestinal distress, visual problems and even death from urinary tract and kidney damage. The essential oil is a powerful abortifacient.

Medicinal Uses: Used today by professionals to treat high blood pressure, heavy periods and tension headaches. Chewing two or three fresh leaves is said to relieve a tension headache almost immediately.

As an antispasmodic, it was once used to treat coughs and colic. Externally, an ointment of Rue may be used to treat rheumatism, gout and sciatica. It is said a compress of Rue placed on the chest is useful for chronic bronchitis. Culpeper recommended heating the juice in the rind of a Pomegranate, then dropping it into painful ears.

Magical Uses: Widely known as a plant of protection – even to non-magical people. The Greeks and even Europeans in the Middle Ages considered it to be a charm against witchcraft and indeed, it is still part of the *Cimaruta* charm found in Italy where it is either worn or placed above the cribs of infants.

The custom of wearing a sprig of Rue around the neck for good health is known as early as 1625 when a Neapolitan physician, Piperno, recommended this practice to treat epilepsy and vertigo.

The juice was used as a protective anointment. Gerard claims, "If a man be anointed with the juice of rue, the poison of wolf's bane, mushrooms, or todestooles, the biting of serpents, springing of scorpions, spiders, bees, hornets and wasps will not hurt him".

Interesting Tidbits: Rue was widely known as an insect repellant. In the Middle Ages (and even beyond) judges would have sprigs of Rue placed around the courtroom to ward off the disease and pestilence brought in from jails by the prisoners.

Rue is an ingredient in Four Thieves' Vinegar, although my personal recommendation is that it should only be so if you are not planning on ingesting your Vinegar.

Rue is not only sacred to Diana but was also consecrated to Hekate.

Pliny said that weasels ate Rue when they were preparing themselves to fight with rats and snakes.

Notes:

Thuja occidentalis
Arbor-Vitae, Thuja

Description: There are five Species in this Genus, native to eastern Asia and North America, four of which are toxic. Often called White or Yellow Cedar, it is *not* a true cedar (*Cedrus spp.*). Arbor-Vitae (Tree of Life) is an evergreen that may grow up to sixty feet high, although cultivated trees rarely reach thirty feet, and approximately two to four feet wide. It is a fast-growing tree and popular for hedges. The leaves are flattened and smell of turpentine when crushed. Minute, yellow-green flowers appear in late spring. Cones, which are green when young then turn a reddish-brown as they mature, are also small and nodding, with overlapping scales.

Cultivation: Thuja grows easily from seed (found inside the cone), planted in autumn. Cuttings may be taken either in spring or autumn. It likes good soil and moderate water in a partially-shady location. If you take cuttings, be sure to mist them frequently.

Parts Used: Aerial.

Poison: All parts of the plant. Toxicity Level I.

Side Effects: The essential oil is a powerful abortifacient. Ingestion may result in fever, headache, gastrointestinal distress, tachycardia, convulsions and damage to the kidneys, heart and liver. Death may result from respiratory or cardiac arrest. Even ingestion of small amounts over a long period of time can be fatal due to the cumulative effects of the thujone content.

Medicinal Uses: Extracts of either the leaves or inner bark are used to treat colds, bronchitis, headaches, rheumatism, fever and cystitis. A decoction of the entire plant is used as a wash for sprains.

Magical Uses: Leaves and twigs are burned and the smoke is used not only to purify sacred objects but also a smudge to ward off evil spirits.

Interesting Tidbits: Thuja wood is used just as Cedar for arrows, spears, boats, furniture, boxes – the list goes on.

Fresh branches are used in Canada as besoms due to the fragrance. Speaking of which, the women of the Chippewa use the leaves as perfume for their clothing. Not only does it smell good, it's a good moth repellant.

T. articulata (a native of northern Africa) is the source of the resin known as Sandarac.

Notes:

SECTION FOUR

Let's Get High

Surely you know by now that anything that makes you drunk or high is the result of inhaling or ingesting a substance that is poisonous to your body. (Hello? In*toxic*ation?) Most of the following are well-known intoxicants but some may surprise you.

Agave tequilana, A. americana
Agave, Century Plant

Description: The Agaves are native to the southwestern United States, Central and South America. *A. tequilana* (Blue Agave) and *A. americana* are the two best known, although there are approximately 208 Species in the Agave Genus. It is a succulent with a large rosette of fleshy leaves with pointed ends and spiny edges. The stem is so short, it appears the leaves grow directly out of the ground. It takes years to flower (sometimes more than ten years) and when it does, it only does so once. A single flower appears on a stem up to forty feet high, growing from the center of the rosette. Once the fruit has matured, the original plant dies but suckers often grow from the base of the stem, yielding new plants. Science still struggles over the plant identification as many Species produce numerous variations.

Cultivation: Agave prefers a very warm climate so if you experience freezing winters, plan on it being a potted plant. It prefers full sun to filtered shade. Although it will tolerate rich soil, it has adapted itself to poor, rocky soil. It is best propagated from suckers (or offsets). Water frequently until new top growth is seen, then reduce to every two weeks during the summer, once a month in spring and fall, and do not water over the winter.

Parts Used: All.

Poison: All parts of the plant. Toxicity Level II.

Side Effects: The spiny edges can cut. The juice is a skin irritant, producing itching and blistering that may reoccur up to a year later. Ingestion may result in irritation of the mucous membranes and/or kidney damage. As the source of mescal, pulque and tequila, intoxication can have disastrous consequences.

Medicinal Uses: The various parts of the plant are used as food by indigenous peoples. The sap has antibacterial properties and can be used to check the growth of bacteria in the stomach and intestines. The juice is a laxative. Soaking the fiber in water results in a tonic that can be used to treat falling hair. A decoction of the root has been used to treat arthritis.

In recent times, "Agave Nectar" or "Agave Syrup" has become popular as a "natural" sweetener. It is lower in glucose than sugar so many diabetics think it is a safe alternative. I would caution anyone considering this to do their research. Commercial Agave Nectar contains as much (or more) fructose than High Fructose Corn Syrup and ingestion of large amounts of fructose may be deleterious to your health.

Magical Uses: None known.

Interesting Tidbits: *A. tequilana* is native to Jalisco, Mexico and those bottles of tequila that say "100% Blue Agave Tequila" are distilled from a particular variety and only in specific Mexican states.

When dried and sliced, the flower stems form natural razor strops. The leaf fiber is used to make sandals, ropes, mats and even linings for cradles. The pointed ends of leaves are used as needles, pens and nails.

The ladies of one Native American tribe use the juice as a face cream. Although not a relative, it probably has the same soothing qualities as Aloe Vera.

Notes:

Amanita muscaria
Fly Agaric, Wart Cap

Description: This is not a plant, *per se*; it is a fungus, but due to its popularity I felt it had to be included. Native to the temperate and boreal regions of the northern hemisphere, it has been introduced in many countries of the southern hemisphere. It can be found as a symbiont in both fir and deciduous forests and is now quite citified. It is the quintessential toadstool: large, white-gilled, with a white-spotted red cap. Some varieties will have a yellow-to-orange-to-olive brown cap but most still have the white spots. Like most mushrooms, it decays quickly after maturity.

Cultivation: Since it is a tree symbiont (it really likes pine but will also grow near other trees), you would have to be very lucky to cultivate Fly Agaric on your own. However, the spores are available from a few online sources and, following their instructions, you may be able to grow your own crop.

Parts Used: The whole thing, technically known as the "fruiting body".

Poison: All parts. Toxicity Level: I. The "Death Cap" *A. phalloides* and "Destroying Angel" *A. virosa* are thought to be the most deadly poisons in the world. One-half of a cap may be fatal and there are no known antidotes.

Side Effects: Depending on the habitat (which dictates the chemical composition) and the amount consumed per body weight, the initial effects may be only slightly hallucinogenic. Other reactions may include nausea, twitching, drowsiness, low blood pressure and excessive salivation. In severe cases, seizures and coma may occur, as well as kidney damage and death from respiratory arrest.

Medicinal Uses: A homeopathic preparation known as "Aga" is used to treat such chronic conditions as chorea and chilblains, as well as to clear up certain cataracts. After extensive preparation, the inner meat was once used by surgeons to arrest bleeding. The toxins in *A. muscaria* are water-soluble and the thinly-sliced, boiled mushroom is consumed as food in various parts of northern Europe, North America, and Japan.

Magical Uses: *A. muscaria* was widely used as an entheogen by the shamans of some indigenous peoples of Siberia. Other unconfirmed accounts tell of its use as an entheogen by the Sami of Finland, some groups in Afghanistan and a few tribes in North America.

The red-and-white toadstool may be seen on Christmas and New Year cards around the world. It is a symbol of good luck.

Interesting Tidbits: The poison, extracted in milk, was once used to kill flies, hence the common name "fly agaric".

A. muscaria has been identified as the *Soma* of ancient India (and mentioned in the Vedic texts), making it possibly the world's oldest hallucinogen.

The active principles in *A. muscaria* pass through the body unmetabolized. A ritual of drinking the urine of someone who ingested the mushroom is mentioned in the Rig-Veda;

this ritual is also found in eastern Siberia where others would drink the shaman's urine after he ingested the fungus. Along the same lines, reindeer will eat Fly Agaric willingly. If one consumes reindeer meat too soon thereafter, the meat will intoxicate the consumer.

Fly Agaric is a common image in popular culture: the familiar red-and-white toadstools may be seen in *The Smurfs*, in the dancing mushroom sequence of *Fantasia*, and in the video game *Super Mario Brothers*.

Notes:

Areca catechu
Betel Nut, Pinang, Siri, Supari

Description: Approximately 60 Species comprise the Genus *Areca*. *A. catechu* is a cultigen (cultivated by Man rather than Nature), growing throughout the tropics of Southeast Asia; it probably was domesticated around 10,000 BCE. It is a slender palm tree, rising up to 75 or 80 feet with long leaves. Male and female flowers appear on the same tree, forming 150-200 oval, yellowish-red fruits about the size of an egg per tree. Each fruit contains one brown seed.

Cultivation: If you live in the tropics, try planting a few seeds. Care for them as you would any member of the palm family.

Parts Used: Seed.

Poison: The seed. Toxicity Level II.

Side Effects: Chewing a nut increases salivation, dulls the appetite and gives a relaxed feeling similar to alcohol intoxication or a nicotine-like high. Indeed, withdrawal symptoms are very similar to withdrawal from nicotine: headache, sweats and tremors. Higher doses may produce excessive sweating, burning in the mouth and throat, bradycardia, tremors, diarrhea and possibly respiratory or cardiac arrest. There is an increased risk of mouth cancer, heart disease and asthma with regular use.

Medicinal Uses: Areca nuts were once used frequently in human medicine. They were considered "gently tonic and powerfully astringent". Therefore, they were prescribed in cases of diarrhea and uterine hemorrhage; the nut powder was snuffed to stop a nosebleed. An extract of the nut is used in veterinary medicine against intestinal worms in cattle and dogs. The same use made it once popular in European tooth powders; powdered nuts are still used in India to treat tapeworms. It is considered an aphrodisiac in many of the countries where it grows: it stimulates available energy and elevates the mood. However, long-term use is said to weaken sexual potency.

Magical Uses: Natives of Borneo used the flowers in charms for healing.

Interesting Tidbits: The seeds are generally ingested as a preparation known as "betel", which is sliced seeds and a bit of lime fruit rolled into a leaf of *Piper betle*. Habitual Betel chewers are easily identified by their red-stained mouth, gums and teeth. They will frequently spit like tobacco chewers, as well, because swallowing one's saliva while chewing the nut will cause nausea.

Notes:

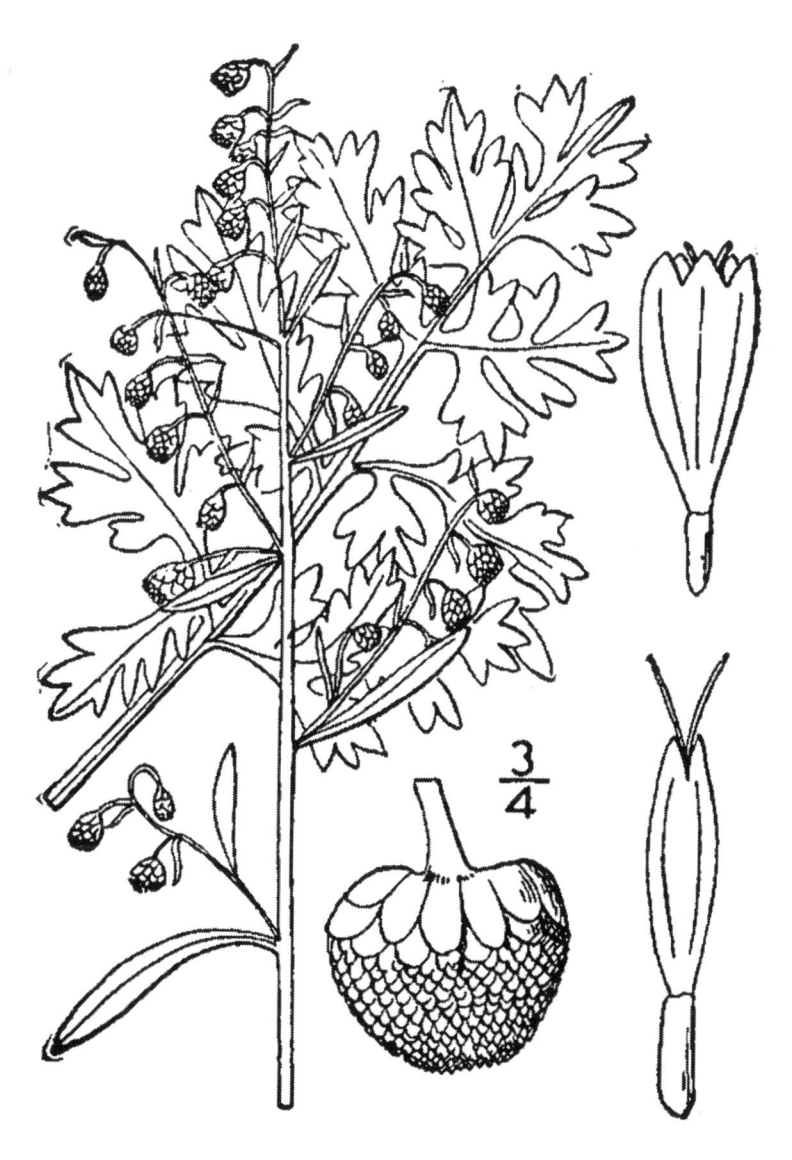

Artemisia absinthium

Artemisia absinthium
Wormwood, Absinthe, Green Ginger, Abrotania

Description: There are more than 350 Species in the Genus *Artemisia*, which was named for the Greek goddess Artemis (the Roman Diana), the goddess of the Moon. This particular Species has a perennial root, from which rise branched leaf stems, sometimes up to five feet high. The foliage is a gray-green which seems to reflect moonlight. The flowers, which appear in late summer, are greenish-yellow and quite small. Wormwood has a tough, almost wood-like stalk and is often grown as a shrub.

Cultivation: Wormwood grows easily from seed or root division. Plant the seeds in the fall as soon as they are ripe. Other than liking shade, it doesn't seem to care about soil composition and is drought-resistant.

Parts Used: Aerial.

Poison: All parts. Toxicity Level II.

Side Effects: In small doses, a mild high. Due to the thujone content, acute poisoning can occur with larger doses. Symptoms include vomiting, strong diarrhea, dizziness, convulsions, coma and possibly death. Chronic consumption causes hallucinations, delirium and seizures.

Medicinal Uses: Large doses are dangerous in many respects, not the least of which it is an abortifacient and has been used as such for centuries. In small doses, it is useful as an appetite stimulant and to relieve flatulence, fever and jaundice. It depresses the area of the brain concerned with pain and anxiety and therefore may be used to temporarily soothe someone with a nervous temperament. Topically, a poultice is used for bruises, sprains and swelling.

Although the toxic nature of Wormwood was known, it was used before the introduction of "Peruvian Bark" (*Cinchona spp.*) to treat malaria and other "intermittents".

Wormwood was once called "Boy's Love" or "Old Man". An ointment was made from the ashes of burned Wormwood and used by young men to promote the growth of a beard.

Magical Uses: Wormwood is burned in incenses used to increase psychic abilities or to call spirits. Pliny said that placing Wormwood under one's pillow would relieve insomnia, or carried would protect the feet from tiredness or becoming hot.

An old love charm: "On St. Luke's Day [October 18th], take marigold flowers, a spring of marjoram, thyme, and a little Wormwood; dry them before a fire, rub them to powder, then sift it through a fine piece of lawn, and simmer it over a slow fire, adding a small quantity of virgin honey, and vinegar. Anoint yourself with this when you go to bed, saying the following lines three times, and you will dream of your partner 'that is to be': St. Luke, St. Luke, be kind to me; In dreams let me my true-love see."

Interesting Tidbits: Has been used for centuries for pest control. A book on husbandry published in 1577 suggests one strew Wormwood to repel fleas; others recommend layering Wormwood with wool and furs to keep away moths and other insects.

Wormwood, along with Rue, is thought to be the bitterest herb known. Despite this, the fresh tops were in wide demand until the early part of the 20th century as an ingredient in beer, rather than hops.

Wormwood essential oil was once an ingredient in Absinthe, an alcoholic drink that was widely popular in the Victorian era. So popular, in fact, that drinking Absinthe was a ritual: a sugar cube was placed onto a specially-slotted spoon and water was poured over the sugar into a glass of Absinthe until one had a ratio of 3-5 parts sugar water to 1 part Absinthe.

Absinthe was banned in many countries, including the United States by 1915, mostly due to the temperance movement alluding to it being psychoactive and dangerous. Indeed, although he may have had other psychological problems, it is thought Van Gogh cut off his ear and finally committed suicide while under the influence of Absinthe. Research has since shown that Absinthe is no more evil than any other spirit and due to the diligence of many fans (and producers) the majority of those laws have now been repealed. One can easily find not only Absinthe but

Wormwood Essential Oil commercially. The fact remains, however, that the essential oil is extremely potent and as little as three teaspoons can cause coma and death.

Notes:

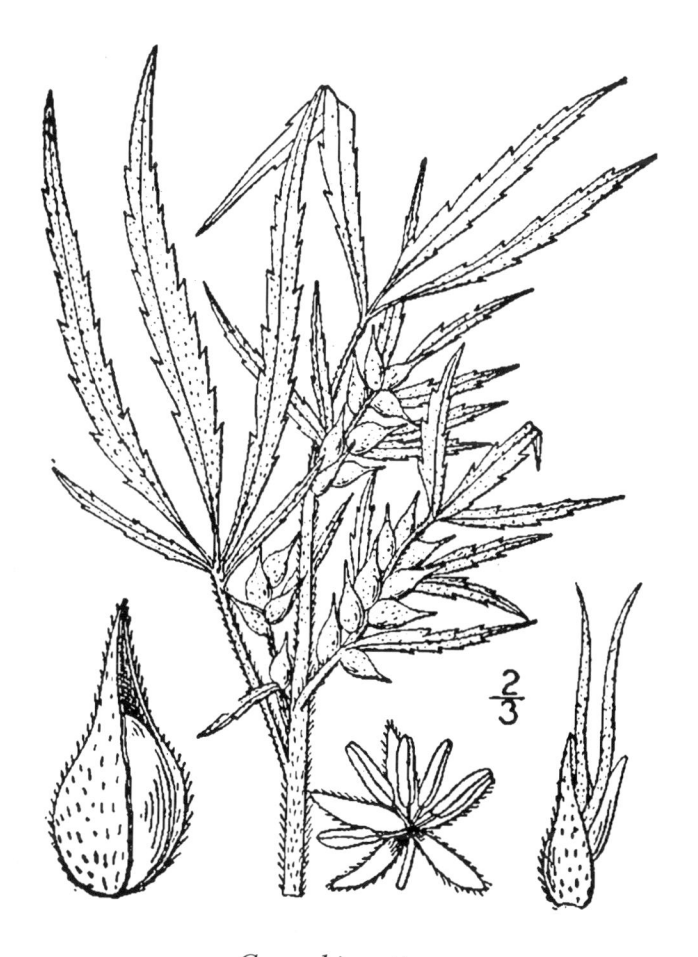

Cannabis sativa

Cannabis sativa
Marijuana, Hemp

Description: A native of the Indian subcontinent, this annual can be found growing wild and cultivated throughout the world in temperate climates, or indoors under grow lights. It has rough, angular, branched stems growing from three to ten feet in height. The leaves have serrated edges, are smooth and dark green on the upper surface, lighter green and slightly hairy on the lower. The flowers, which appear in late summer to early fall, are small and green. The fruit is small, ash colored and completely filled by the seed.

Cultivation: I'm not going to discuss the legalities of growing hemp or marijuana here. Suffice it to say that Cannabis requires a neutral-to-slightly-acidic soil, full sun and a moderate amount of water. It is subject to root rot if overwatered.

Parts Used: Flowering tops (marijuana); resin (hashish); aerial (industrial hemp).

Poison: All parts. Toxicity Level III.

Side Effects: In small doses, a moderate, short-lasting high that is relaxant in nature. High doses may produce paranoia and anxiety. Industrial hemp is usually a strain that has had the majority of THC bred out of it and rarely produces any symptoms if smoked or ingested.

Medicinal Uses: In parts of the United States and in other countries, marijuana is approved as a medicinal drug for glaucoma, nausea (when produced by chemotherapy) and as an appetite stimulant for AIDS patients. The ancients used it to treat general pain, rheumatism, and asthma.

In the Middle Ages, it was pounded with lard and applied for pain or swelling of the breast. It was also infused in water for 24 hours and then combed through the hair to make it grow.

As late as the early 20th century, Cannabis was prescribed in various forms for easing pain, inducing sleep, soothing nervous disorders, neuralgia, gout, infantile convulsions, gonorrhea, and a prolapsed uterus.

It is said that hashish (the resin) was used in China as early as 220 CE as a sedative for surgery.

The Iroquois use it as a psychological aid and stimulant; Persian soldiers in the Crusades used it to produce fanaticism.

Culpeper warned, "too much use of it dries up the seed for procreation".

Magical Uses: The Assyrians used Cannabis as an incense in the 9th century BCE.

From Guernsey in the 1880's comes a spell for love divination: "A vision of your future husband can be obtained by the sowing of hemp seed. The young maiden must scatter on the ground saying, "Hemp-seed I sow, Hemp-seed grow, For my true love to come and mow". Having done this, she must immediately run into the house and looking back she will see her lover mowing the hemp, which has grown rapidly and mysteriously."

Interesting Tidbits: In Shakespeare's time, hemp was called "neckweed", referencing the hempen ropes used at the gallows.

In India, tradition maintains that the gods sent Hemp so man might attain delight, courage, and have heightened sexual desire. It is consecrated to Shiva and was Indra's favorite drink ("nectar dropping from heaven").

Herodotus wrote approximately 430 BCE that the Scythians (8th century BCE to 2nd century CE) used a tent and hemp seeds on hot stones as a substitute for an ordinary bath.

Galen wrote about 220 CE that Cannabis was given to party guests to promote hilarity and enjoyment.

Although a native of India, Cannabis made its way to the United States quite early on – legend holds that Christopher Columbus delivered it to our shores in 1492. Due to the fibers (not just the intoxicating qualities), it became a huge cash crop, becoming America's third largest crop (behind tobacco and corn) in 1850.

Two or three green sprigs placed in beds will drive bedbugs away.

The fruit (akene) is edible and nutritious.

Notes:

Cola spp.
Kola Nut

Description: There are approximately 100 Species in this Genus, the most common being *Cola vera* which is a native of West Africa and is cultivated in other tropical climates. Kola is an evergreen tree that grows up to sixty feet high. Its leaves are six to eight inches long, ovate with points at each end. The flowers are yellow and spotted with purple. The fruit is star-shaped and the "nut" is the seed pod.

Cultivation: Kola requires a hot, humid climate but will withstand some dry conditions as long as it gets a lot of water. Originally found in tropical rainforests, some Species will tolerate partly-sunny conditions while others prefer shade. If planted outdoors rather than in a hothouse, a windbreak is required in areas where strong winds are experienced. It also doesn't like to share its ground with anyone else so requires a weed-free environment.

Parts Used: The nut (seed pod).

Poison: The seed. Toxicity Level: III.

Side Effects: Kola's stimulant effects are very similar to caffeine. Just as with other caffeinated products, overuse can lead to nervousness, insomnia and addiction.

Medicinal Uses: As well as a stimulant, Kola also has a very astringent effect. It has been used as a nervine and heart tonic in Europe and a Kola drink is used in Jamaica and Brazil as a sexual stimulant. The powdered seeds are used as a digestive in many parts of Africa and the West Indies, and sometimes used to treat pertussis and asthma. It is also used topically to aid in the healing of cuts.

Magical Uses: In parts of West Africa Kola is used as a sacred offering during prayers and other significant life events. Particularly in Nigeria, the Igbo use the Kola nut in a ceremony to welcome guests to the village or home. Kola nuts are an integral part of a divination system known as "Obi", which is practiced in West Africa and other parts of the world, most often by those of the Yoruba religion.

Interesting Tidbits: The well-known soft drink, Coca-Cola, was invented by a pharmacist in Georgia in the 1800's from extracts of kola and coca, and other ingredients. Cocaine was prohibited in soft drinks in the United States by 1904, yet it is rumored (the recipe is still a closely-guarded secret) that Kola extract is an ingredient to this day. Kola extract can also be found in other soft drinks, most notably a sweet drink known as "Clayton's Kola Tonic" in Barbados.

Some African Muslims chew a Kola nut for its stimulant effects because they are forbidden to drink alcohol.

Notes:

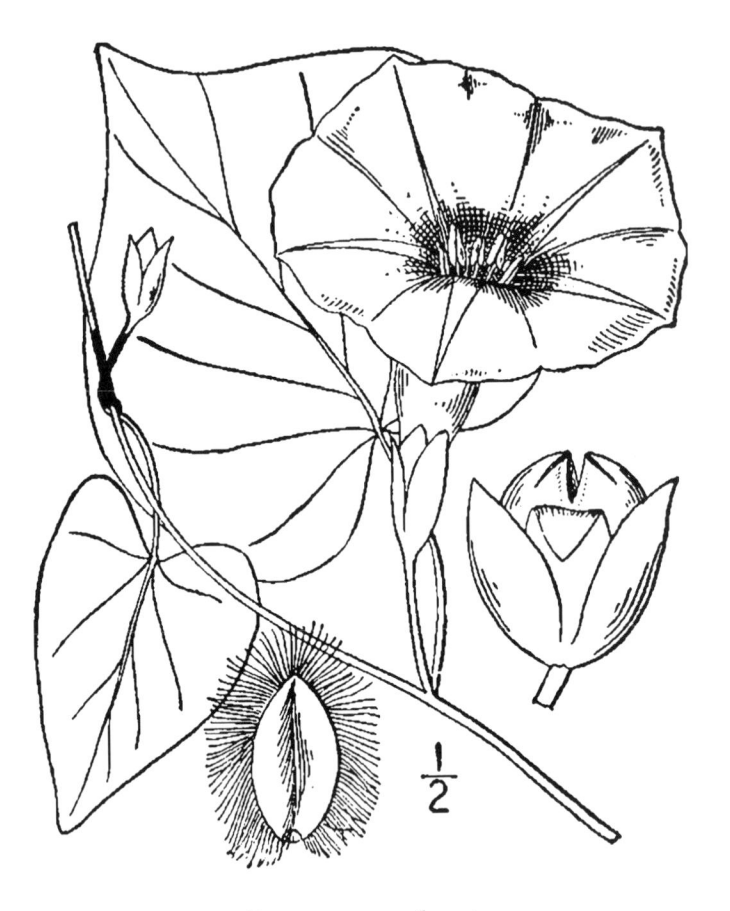

Ipomoea pandurata

Convolvulus spp., Ipomea spp.
Morning Glory, Jalap, High John the Conqueror, Bindweed

Description: There is confusion in the plant world! Originally, all "Bindweeds" were grouped under one Convolvulus Species. Within the last century, some were split out into the Ipomea Species. They are all members of the Convolvulaceae family, which has more than 1,650 Species under its individual tribes. Because of the confusion and synonyms, I'm grouping both Genera into one entry.

Generally speaking, members of the *Convolvulaceae* Family have very deep roots and delicate, creeping stems that will twine around most anything within reach. The common name of the Family (and many Species), Bindweed, is very apt as these plants do not support themselves by tendrils but wind themselves tightly around the object which supports it. They are either annual or perennial, producing flowers from early summer through autumn. The flowers are individual, trumpet-shaped and nearly every color of the rainbow, depending on Species.

Cultivation: They are native to tropical and subtropical regions of the world but are cultivated and even naturalized over the majority of the world – in some parts they are considered invasive and noxious weeds. They grow easily from seed and will propagate themselves via underground runners from the main root. Most Species tolerate full sun and even poor soil.

Parts Used: Medicinally, the root.

Poison: The seeds. Toxicity Level II.

Side Effects: Roots of some of the *Convolvulus* Species are purgative and in some cases, a *strong* one. Ingestion of seeds, especially those of the *Ipomea* Genus, may cause high heart rates, frightening hallucinations (sometimes described as an LSD-type experience), nausea and abortion.

Medicinal Uses: The tuber of *Convolvulus batatas* is a very nourishing food: you'll know it better as a Sweet Potato.

As late as the 1930's, a drug known as "Jalap" was commercially produced from a resin in the root of *C. jalapa* (synonym *Ipomea purga*) for the treatment of constipation and was considered safe enough for children (sweetening the preparation with sugar to disguise the taste). It is still used as a homemade medicine today. A more drastic purgative, Scammony, was also produced from the root of a related Species.

A tincture of the flowers of Morning Glory (exact Latin binomial unknown) was once used for headaches, rheumatism and to help "inflamed" eyes.

The root of *C. arvensis* is used by the Navajo both internally and externally to treat spider bites; the Pomo take a decoction to treat metrorrhagia.

Magical Uses: The seeds of *I. tricolor* are ingested by Mazatec curanderas to obtain information about illnesses and to locate lost objects; those who are untrained and under its influence are said to talk with dead relatives and give away secrets.

The root of *I. purga*, known as High John the Conqueror in some circles, is used for binding, commanding, courage, overcoming obstacles, protection and purification.

Interesting Tidbits: In 1651, the Physician to the King of Spain reportedly used the "Aztec root" to cure syphilis and mitigate pain caused by chills; others used this root to relieve flatulence and remove tumors.

Morning Glory seeds were used by Aztec priests in a body rub to make their sacrificial victims "fearless". This suggests the hallucinogenic properties of Morning Glory can be absorbed through the skin.

Notes:

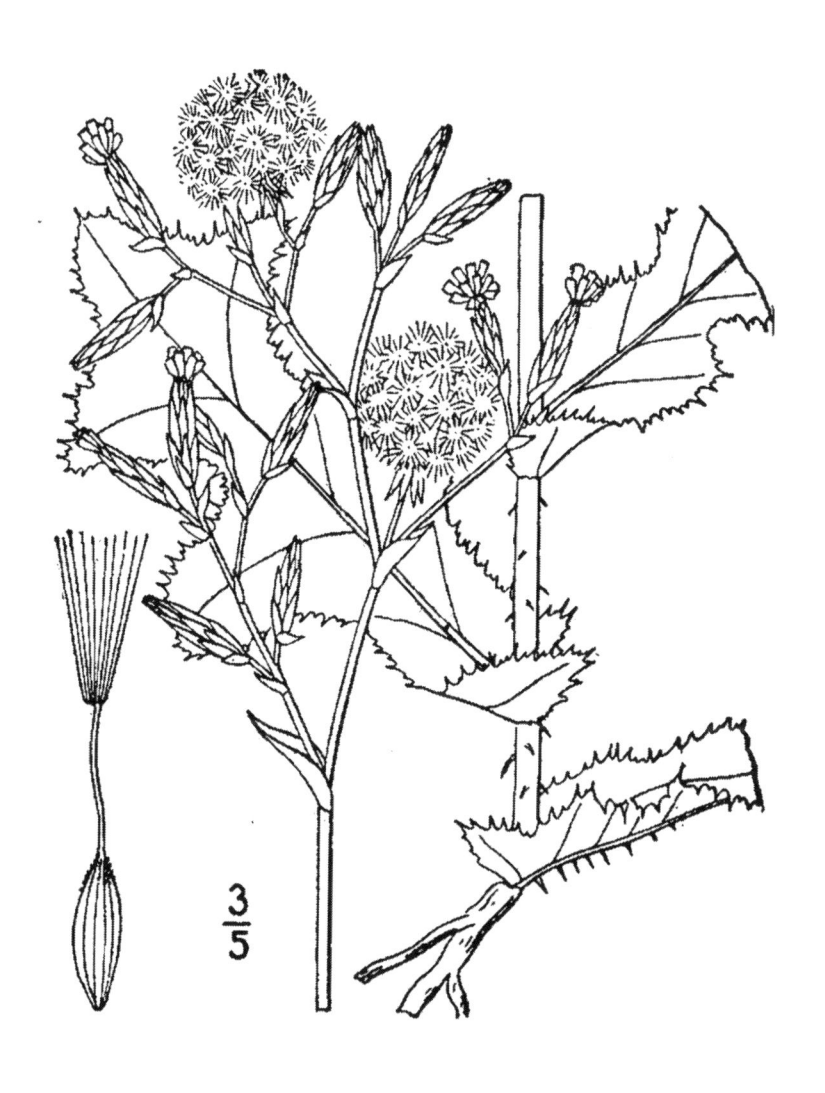

Lactuca virosa

Lactuca virosa
Wild Lettuce, Opium Lettuce

Description: A native of Western and Southern Europe, Wild Lettuce is a biennial plant that bears little resemblance to "garden" lettuce. It produces a simple rosette of leaves in its first year and shoots up a stalk to a height of six or seven feet in its second year with a tall, erect, somewhat prickly stem and rather large, oblong leaves. The flowers are generally yellow and appear in July and August, followed by a rough, black fruit. The entire plant is full of a milky white juice (latex).

Cultivation: Wild Lettuce grows on banks and in waste places throughout its native habitat and indeed, wherever British colonists set foot. As with garden lettuce, it will grow from seed. Press the seeds into moist soil (no need to cover) and water. Germination happens in a couple of weeks. It prefers rich soil and full sun but as it grows in "waste places" – soil consideration isn't a priority. It will readily reseed itself.

Parts Used: The leaves, gathered in the second year before the flowers open.

Poison: All parts but especially the latex. Toxicity Level I.

Side Effects: With moderate use, produces euphoria and happiness, followed by a sedating and analgesic effect. Indeed, Maud Grieve said, "The drug resembles a feeble opium". Higher doses lead to excessive perspiration, heart palpitations, distorted vision, vertigo and possibly death.

Medicinal Uses: It was formerly used in medicine as an opium substitute. The sap was collected, dried, rolled into balls and sold as "lactucarium" and one may still find people today who smoke it similarly to opium. Culpeper recommended a syrup made with Wild Lettuce as an anodyne, saying it "gently disposes patients to sleep without the violent effects of other opiates". Even today, one may find suggestions of an infusion of the leaves to help with coughs, bronchitis, and insomnia.

An infusion of leaves is used by the Navajo to treat gastroenteritis.

Magical Uses: The leaves were used in medieval love potions and charms; and it was said to promote child-bearing in women.

There are those who suggest that smoking the dried sap before bed will enhance the vividness of one's dreams.

Interesting Tidbits: The sap contains up to 60% latex, an ingredient in rubber. This sap was experimented with during World War II as an alternative source for rubber with which to make tires. They couldn't, however, seem to grow enough lettuce to make this a viable alternative and the industry failed.

During the Victorian Era, it was thought eating or drinking a decoction of the seeds would "hindreth generation of seed and venereous imaginations". (Translation: It would make a man sterile and reduce sexual desire.) As it's a sedative, it's no surprise that it would reduce sexual desire (it's also used to treat nymphomania) but making a man sterile has no basis in scientific fact.

Notes:

Papaver somniferum

Papaver somniferum
Opium Poppy

Description: There are approximately 80 Species of *Papaver*. *P. somniferum* is a native of Asia Minor but one can find this and other Species growing throughout the world, even as ornamentals in someone's garden. It is an erect annual, with toothed, hairless leaves and flowers varying in color from pure white to reddish purple. All parts of the plant contain a system of vessels filled with a white latex.

Cultivation: Although cultivation of *P. somniferum* is illegal in the United States and Canada (and probably elsewhere), other Species are available as garden ornamentals or for the culinary use of poppy seeds. While not as strong as the Opium Poppy, they do contain some of the narcotic chemicals. Although planting in the fall for a spring crop is preferred, they will not overwinter in a climate where below-zero (F) temperatures are normal. In that case, wait until spring to plant. Plant in loamy or sandy soil with a slightly acidic pH and lightly cover. Keep moist (but not wet) while germination takes place, which will be in a week or so. They will tolerate slightly dry conditions and indeed, once flowers have appeared, do not water unless absolutely necessary. They do not readily reseed themselves but produce plenty so you'll have not only enough to cook with but to plant for another crop.

Parts Used: For cooking: the seed. For other uses: the latex found throughout the plant but in most abundance in the capsule.

Poison: The latex. Toxicity Level I.

Side Effects: Ingestion or inhalation of the latex induces euphoria but also depresses the respiratory system and interferes with the endorphin receptors in the brain. Overdosing produces respiratory arrest, leading to death.

While legal, eating a poppy-seed bun may produce a positive drug test.

Medicinal Uses: Known since Antiquity for its sedating and mind-altering properties. Even today, various preparations (either natural or synthetic) of opium are used as painkillers, not only at home but within the medical community. In some indigenous cultures, an infusion is used to treat teething in babies. *P. somniferum* is also astringent and was once used to treat diarrhea and dysentery.

In Medieval times, the latex was mixed with vinegar and smeared on the face to treat a headache.

Due to its various chemical constituents, all of which are pain-killing, the Opium Poppy is the most prescribed poisonous plant on Earth.

Magical Uses: The Poppy is sacred to Demeter and features in many of her mysteries. A cake baked with poppy seeds is an appropriate gift to her.

The seeds were thought to ward off evil spirits (and witches). This is another story wherein they had to count something – in this case, seeds – that would take so long they'd not have time to do their evil deeds.

An indigenous tribe of Poland scattered seeds in the coffin to ward off vampires.

In some parts of England, the flowers were placed among roof timbers to keep lightning from hitting the house.

Interesting Tidbits: Poppy seeds have been found in excavations in Switzerland and Scotland, showing their use in the Neolithic and Bronze Ages.

At the Battle of Agra (c. 1713), the Rajputa, a hereditary race of warriors, ate opium in copious quantities, making them insensible to danger. (My question is, how did they stay awake to fight?)

Opium trade with China was big business in England and the British Colonies during the Victorian Era. Spats between the East India Company and the Chinese purveyors sparked the "Opium Wars" between England and China (1839-1842 and 1856-1860).

The ancient Greeks venerated the Opium Poppy so much that it was dedicated to a number of gods for a number of reasons, the most obvious being a dedication to Hypnos (the god of sleep) and Morpheus, his son, the god of dreams.

It is said the Genus name, *Papaver* was given because the latex was mixed with pap (a kind of porridge) and given to children to make them go to sleep.

Even today, young plants (that are pulled to prevent crowding) are used as pot-herbs where the Opium Poppy is cultivated as a crop.

Notes:

Pausinystalia yohimbe
Yohimbe

Description: Yohimbe is an evergreen tree native to the tropical forests of western Africa. It can grow to a height of nearly one hundred feet with light brown or gray-brown bark, and bears a slight resemblance to an Oak. Its leaves are oval but unlike the Oak, it produces winged seeds.

Cultivation: *Requires* a tropical to semi-tropical climate. For the majority of the readers of this book, Yohimbe will do best as a potted plant in a hothouse and in ideal conditions, will grow to perhaps fifty feet in height. Plant your seeds in a loamy soil, covering them to a depth of about three times the diameter of the seeds. The pots should be placed in a sunny location and watered at least every day, keeping the soil moist but not wet. Be sure to completely drain the soil to prevent the seeds and subsequent roots from rotting.

Parts Used: The bark.

Poison: The bark. Toxicity Level I.

Side Effects: The dried bark is a central nervous system stimulant and mild hallucinogen. When smoked, the effects are reported to produce a mild euphoria in both sexes and in higher doses, produce effects similar to those of LSD. Ingestion stimulates the spinal ganglia, resulting in an erection in males.

Yohimbe is an MAO inhibitor and combined with other similar drugs or alcohol, can cause a dangerous drop in blood pressure; or combined with amphetamines, a dangerous spike in blood pressure.

Seizures and renal failure have also been reported.

Medicinal Uses: The bark has been used for centuries by those for whom it is a native plant to treat sexual impotence. A standardized version of the extract is available by prescription for treatment of erectile and orgasmic dysfunction in men.

Other uses include treatment of hyposexual disorder in women and as a blood pressure boosting agent for certain diseases. It was once explored as a remedy for Type 2 diabetes but those explorations were abandoned due to the many complications of combining Yohimbe with other drugs.

In therapeutic settings, Yohimbine (the chemical extract) has been used to facilitate memory recall in patients with Post Traumatic Stress Disorder.

Numerous bodybuilding companies sell transdermal formulations that include Yohimbine that, in theory, will help with fat loss in athletes. There is, however, little clinical evidence to support this claim.

Magical Uses: None specifically, although it is and has been used in sex magic rituals, most notably by Aleister Crowley. It is also used as a sacrament in some pagan wedding ceremonies.

Many indigenous people of western Africa use Yohimbe bark in ritual: the Bantu use it in mating ritual; the Masai mix Yohimbe with other herbs and use it in their warrior initiation ritual.

In Cameroon, it is thought male impotence stems from black magic and it is used in their folk medicine as a treatment for such.

Interesting Tidbits: The active chemicals, alkaloids, can only be extracted from the bark after it is dried and is generally taken from trees fifteen to twenty years old.

The tree is threatened with extinction in its native habitat due to demand for the bark.

While the standardized extract requires a prescription in the United States, as of this writing the bark is still legal, although considered "unsafe" by the Food and Drug Administration. The trade of Yohimbe bark *has* been banned by other governments, including Canada, Australia and the United Kingdom.

Mixing 500-1,000 mg Vitamin C into a Yohimbe infusion will mitigate the nauseous effects.

Notes:

Turnera diffusa
Damiana, Mexican Holly

Description: There are approximately fifty Species in this Genus and all are slightly hazardous. *T. diffusa* and *T. aphrodisiaca* are generally regarded as the same plant. They are a small, perennial shrub native to the American Southwest, Mexico, Central and South America, and the West Indies. They grow up to six feet high and have smooth, pale green leaves with a few hairs on the ribs. Single yellow flowers appear in July or August, giving way to a fragrant, fig-like fruit.

Cultivation: Damiana prefers full sun and a rich soil. It will only tolerate freezing temperatures for a short time so if you live north of zone 9 in the United States, you may want to keep this one in a greenhouse. If you live in zone 9 or farther south, sow the seeds directly on top of the soil during fall or winter. While the seeds are readily available for collection from the seed pods, it is easily propagated by cuttings.

Parts Used: Leaves.

Poison: The leaves. Toxicity Level: III.

Side Effects: Damiana is usually smoked as a mild aphrodisiac and euphoric, producing effects similar to those of Marijuana. It can also be a mild purgative. Damiana has a mild hypoglycemic effect and should be used with caution by those who have diabetes or hypoglycemia. It has a traditional use as an abortifacient and should be avoided by pregnant women.

Medicinal Uses: An infusion is typically used by those who live where it is native as a tonic, especially for the sexual organs and nervous system. It has been used by indigenous cultures since time immemorial and studied and used in Western medicine for at least 100 years: the leaf and "elixir" were listed in the National Formulary in the United States from 1888 to 1947.

The list of indicated conditions for its use by indigenous cultures is about as long as my arm ... in other words, for just about anything.

T. diffusa is being studied for the treatment of breast cancer, although this is still in the research phase – it may also *do further harm* to those who already have breast cancer.

Damiana is used homeopathically for the treatment of anxiety, depression, nervousness and to regulate hormones.

Magical Uses: None specifically, although it has been used since ancient times, most notably the Maya and Aztecs, as a stimulant and aphrodisiac. Even today, Mexican women will take a cup of infusion one or two hours prior to intercourse to help immerse themselves in the act.

Interesting Tidbits: Mexican folklore claims that Damiana was used in the *original* recipe for a Margarita. Today, Damiana Liqueur is made only from *T. diffusa* growing in Baja California; it's used in place of Triple Sec.

Notes:

SECTION FIVE

Really Awful

While every plant on this planet has *some* use, this last section comprises some of the meanest there are. Just a taste can cause agony or even death.

Abrus precatorius
Rosary Pea

Description: A native of India, it is a perennial vine. The stem is woody with smooth brown bark and light green, pinnate leaves. The flowers are white, pink, or light purple and so small as to go almost unnoticed. The pods contain four or five brightly-colored seeds, usually red or black but sometimes white.

Cultivation: Requires a tropical climate. Scarify seeds then soak in hot water overnight. Those that swell may be planted in relatively rich soil, covering with dirt two to three times the height of the seed. Ensure plenty of water and sun but do not water in the winter.

Parts Used: All parts.

Poison: The seeds. Toxicity Level I.

Side Effects: The seed contains a toxin similar to but more deadly than Ricin. Symptoms appear several hours after ingestion and include bloody diarrhea and vomiting, hemorrhage, delirium, convulsions and coma. Death occurs three to four days after ingestion from heart failure. If chewed well, one seed is enough to cause death, especially in children.

Medicinal Uses: In India, a tea is made from the leaf to treat fevers, coughs and colds. The seeds are treated prior to using them in various preparations for headaches, diarrhea, fever, malaria, night-blindness, nephritis, and wounds. A paste is made of the seed and leaves, the juice is extracted and then applied once a day to slow down the graying of hair.

In both India and various parts of Africa, the seed is used as an abortifacient or as an oral contraceptive.

Magical Uses: The roots of *A. precatorius* are mixed with black pepper and ginger, then taken to get rid of evil spirits or the effects of black magic; a piece of the root is tied to the arm for more immediate results.

Interesting Tidbits: Despite the toxic nature of the seeds, they are used as beads in necklaces, toys, musical instruments and as decoration. As the toxin is *inside* the seed, they are more dangerous to jewelry makers than wearers, although necklaces are known to cause dermatitis.

The seeds were used in trials by ordeal in the Middle Ages. Whoever survived eating one of the seeds would be declared the victor. Many times, the favored contestant was tipped off beforehand and swallowed the seed whole while his opponent would chew.

Notes:

Cerbera odollam
Suicide Tree

Description: Approximately four Species comprise this Genus, widely distributed in India, Southeast Asia, Australia and the Pacific Islands. Like its cousin, Oleander, it is a small to medium height evergreen shrub or tree, growing up to 45 feet but generally found much shorter. Spirally-arranged leaves set off small, white star-shaped flowers that appear in clusters. The fruit develops singly and is round or oval with a hard cover. They are green when they first appear but turn pink then black as they mature. The seed coat is thin and decays rapidly, exposing fibrous tissue. It appears to both flower and fruit year-round.

Cultivation: It prefers tropical heat and swampy or marshy areas in its native habitat. Therefore, plant outdoors if you live in a tropical climate or keep as a potted plant indoors. Push the seed into the soil so two-thirds of it is still exposed. Water frequently and give it plenty of sun.

Parts Used: All parts.

Poison: The seeds. Toxicity Level I.

Side Effects: Nausea, vomiting, excess salivation, exhaustion and all effects associated with cardiac glycoside poisoning – arrhythmia, hypertension, coma, cardiac arrest. Death may occur within just a few minutes if a concentrated amount is ingested.

Medicinal Uses: The seed oil is used externally as a remedy for scabies and rheumatism. The bark, latex and roots are used in various preparations as purgatives.

Magical Uses: None known.

Interesting Tidbits: It really should be known as the "Suicide and Homicide Tree". Although bitter, the taste of a crushed seed can be easily disguised in sweet or spicy foods. In India, about 75% of fatal poisonings are women and authorities suspect most of these are young wives who do not meet the exacting standards of Indian families.

Cerberin, a relative of the alkaloid digoxin (digitalis), is often difficult to detect in autopsies.

This is another "trial by ordeal" plant and was used extensively as such on the island of Madagascar. Although the practice was outlawed in 1861, it is suspected it may still occur in remote areas.

The wood is used to make colorful masks in Sri Lanka.

The dried drupes (seed coverings) are sold in the potpourri trade as "mintola balls".

The oil is used as an insecticide and repellant and is being investigated for possible conversion to biodiesel.

Notes:

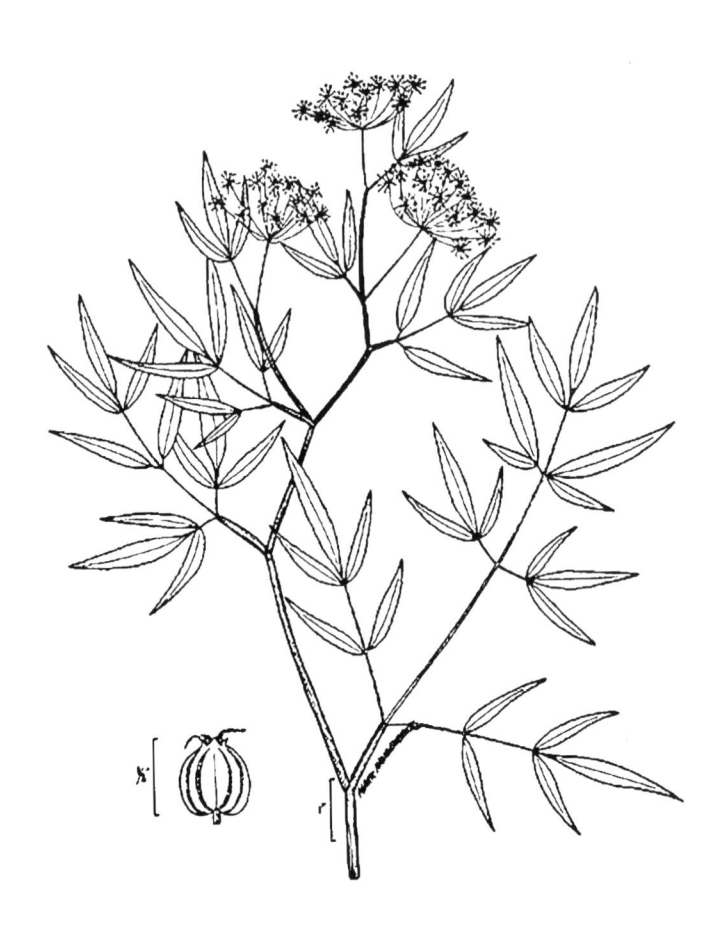

Cicuta maculatum

Cicuta spp.
Water Hemlock, Poison Parsley, Cowbane

Description: There are four Species in the *Cicuta* Genus, all native to Europe, Asia and North America. It is a semi-aquatic plant, usually found growing wild in ditches and along the banks of rivers. It's a perennial herb, rising from a parsnip-shaped root with thick rhizomes. The stems are erect, hollow and may grow as high as four feet. The branches are smooth and slightly furrowed and bear triangular leaves. White flowers appear during the summer, formed in umbels. *C. maculata* is often known as "Spotted Water Hemlock" due to purple spots or stripes found on the stem. It is often confused with true Hemlock, Queen Anne's Lace, Parsley or Angelica.

Cultivation: As its name suggests, this plant prefers a moist but not continually wet environment. Seeds germinate easily in a partial- to full-sun location. *Cicuta* Species are considered invasive in many parts of the world as once established, they are difficult to eradicate.

Parts Used: All parts.

Poison: All parts. Toxicity Level I.

Side Effects: Ingestion causes a burning sensation in the mouth and throat, nausea, vomiting, headache, abdominal pain, strong convulsions, seizures, bradycardia, coma, paralysis and death from respiratory arrest.

Medicinal Uses: Although the toxicity is known, preparations of Water Hemlock are used to treat migraine headaches, dysmenorrhea and intestinal worms. Some Native American tribes use the root internally for contraceptive purposes. A poultice of the root is applied to alleviate skin inflammation and "painful bones" (probably arthritis or rheumatism). A decoction of the entire plant is used as a bath to bring down fevers.

Homeopathically, *Cicuta* preparations are used to treat people with various ailments such as convulsions, concussion and eczema-like skin eruptions.

Magical Uses: None specifically found in western magical traditions but probably similar to True Hemlock *Conium maculatum*. The Ojibwa of North America smoke the root for hunting medicine to draw the buck within arrow range.

Interesting Tidbits: Used by several Native American tribes for poison arrows – not just for hunting but for warfare.

Culpeper, in his *Complete Herbal* (published as *The English Physician* in 1652) states, "Poisonous Water Hemlock, *Cicuta virosa*, and Thick Water Hemlock, are but accidental variations which situation and soil naturally produce, they are thought to be poisonous, but there is nothing certain on this head."

Notes:

Colchicum autumnale

Colchicum autumnale
Meadow Saffron, Autumn Crocus

Description: More than 65 Species comprise the *Colchicum* Genus, which are native to Europe, northern Africa and central Asia. The root (called a corm) produces long, spear-like leaves and fruit in the spring. After the leaves die back in summer, pink-to-purple flowers appear in the fall. They are very popular as ornamental plants.

Cultivation: Prefers a light soil that has been enriched. Plant the bulbs in the fall in a moist bed that is situated where it will get partial sun (under tree shade is good). It is also easily propagated by bulb division. If you are lucky enough to get seeds, start them in a cold frame outdoors, transplanting the seedlings when they are two years old. Plants started from seed will not flower until they are four or five years old.

Parts Used: Root and seed.

Poison: All parts but especially the seeds and bulbs. Toxicity Level I. The bulbs are somewhat sweet and resemble an onion.

Side Effects: Ingestion starts a process which begins with nausea and vomiting, followed by bloody diarrhea, abdominal pain, hypotension, convulsions and paralysis. Lethal doses cause cardiac arrest and cardiovascular collapse. Death generally takes a few days.

Medicinal Uses: In small doses, preparations from the root are used to treat rheumatism and gout. Larger doses are used as an emetic.

Culpeper mentions that a syrup (presumably made from the seed) succeeds where all other expectorants fail.

An herbal from the Middle Ages says to mix the root with oil to clear up acne. Specifically, it "cleans pimples from a woman's nose".

Magical Uses: None known.

Interesting Tidbits: The toxicity of *Colchicum* was mentioned in Assyrian texts (approximately 2500 – 605 BCE).

Nicander (2nd century BCE) called it the "loathsome fire of Colchian Medea". The Genus name is from the Greek *kolkhikon* 'of Colchis', referencing her legendary skills as a poisoner.

The flowers are occasionally used in floral arrangements. However, the water in which the leaves and/or flowers stand then becomes poisonous itself.

This is another murder/suicide plant. Theophrastus (371-287 BCE) said that slaves would take it to commit suicide and its use in murders and suicide attempts is still recorded in Europe.

Notes:

Dieffenbachia spp.
Dieffenbachia, Dumb Cane

Description: About 20 Species are in this Genus, all native to tropical America and generally found as houseplants throughout the world. It's a sturdy plant with long (up to three feet), oval leaves growing on a stout cane. The leaves may be solid green, solid cream or green with cream spots or markings, depending on the Species. Houseplants will rarely flower but outdoors, a green or white spathe will open to reveal a spadix that produces white or yellow flowers.

Cultivation Indoors, a large pot with moist, relatively rich potting soil will produce the largest plant. As it's native to the tropics, it should be watered frequently and daily misting will give it the humidity it likes. It prefers partial sun so near a window is a good spot. Plant outdoors only in zone nine or above, in a slightly shady spot.

Parts Used: Leaves.

Poison: All parts but especially the cane. Toxicity Level I.

Side Effects: Chewing any part of the plant will initially produce a burning sensation in the mouth and throat, following by swelling of the tongue and esophagus. This can lead to loss of speech at best and suffocation at worst. Severe poisoning may lead to coma and death by cardiac arrest or deadly kidney damage. Getting the sap in your eye will cause extreme pain and possibly conjunctivitis or keratitis.

Medicinal Uses: Preparations have been used for contraceptive and aphrodisiac purposes. Traditional medicine has also used it to treat cancer and some skin disorders.

Magical Uses: In Brazil, the plant is used to ward off negative energies and the evil eye. Because of this, it is combined with several other plants in a "seven lucky herbs vase".

Interesting Tidbits: Slave owners in the West Indies would force unruly slaves to chew a piece of Dieffenbachia.

Rumor has it the Nazis investigated the use of a Dieffenbachia extract as a sterilization measure.

Notes:

Euonymus spp.
Euonymus, Spindle Tree, Wahoo

Description: This Genus has about 175 Species, all native to northern temperate zones, as well as a few in Australia. *E. europaeus* is native to Europe and western Asia. It is a deciduous shrub or small tree with green twigs and bright green leaves. The flowers are tiny and white, giving way to showy, red fruit that bursts to expose orange seeds. Its yellow-green to reddish-purple fall color makes it popular as an ornamental plant.

Cultivation: Many Species may be found in garden centers. Propagation is easiest by semi-hardwood cuttings. Plant in well-drained soil in sun or partial shade. Most Species are frost-resistant.

Parts Used: Wood, root bark.

Poison: All parts, especially the fruit. Toxicity Level I.

Side Effects: Toxic symptoms appear ten to eighteen hours after ingestion and include nausea, spasms, bloody diarrhea, arrhythmia, tachycardia, kidney and liver damage, paralysis, coma and death.

Medicinal Uses: *E. atropupurpeus* (native to North America) was popular as a diuretic drug in the nineteenth century. Several Species have also been used as cardiac tonics, expectorants and laxatives. It was also recommended in cases of congestion or fever, and used as a supplement to quinine when treating malaria. The fruit was used in an ointment to kill lice.

Magical Uses: An infusion of the bark is used as a wash to confer courage and is also used by some Native American tribes and Hoodoo workers to break hexes.

Interesting Tidbits: The common name, Spindle Tree, comes from the fact that the wood is so hard it forms a sharp point when carved and was used as wool spindles. It's also been used to make violin bows.

The wood has also been used to make charcoal used in the manufacture of gunpowder.

The seeds yield a yellow dye that was once used to color butter.

Notes:

Gelsemium sempervirens

Gelsemium spp.
Gelsemium, Yellow Jessamine

Description: Only three Species populate this Genus, and all three are equally deadly. Two are native to North America, one to Asia. They are all – supposedly – evergreen vines found not only in woodlands but in gardens worldwide. (Mine dies back in the winter.) The woody stems will grow twenty feet or more in length and twine themselves around anything they can find, including reaching out from tree to tree. The leaves are dark green above and pale green below. Flowers are small, trumpet-like and yellow, appearing in spring.

Cultivation: Divide the rootball and plant at least six feet apart. Seed pods should be allowed to dry on the vine, then broken open; seeds may be planted in the spring in moist soil. It will easily spread via underground runners and is considered invasive in many areas and by many gardeners.

Parts Used: Rhizome.

Poison: All parts, especially the roots and nectar. Toxicity Level I.

Side Effects: Initial symptoms are enlarging of the pupils, followed by muscular weakness and hypotension. It has sedative effects and a sensation of languor has been reported. Death is due to respiratory arrest.

Medicinal Uses: A tincture has been used in the past in cases of neuralgia, especially facial pain arising from decaying teeth or damaged nerves. Extracts have also been used to treat fevers, in cough syrups and for bleeding hemorrhoids.

Magical Uses: None known.

Interesting Tidbits: *G. elegans* is used in China and Japan to execute criminals, and it's traditionally used for murder or suicide in Malaysia.

G. sempervirens, also commonly known as Carolina Jessamine (or Jasmine) is the state flower of South Carolina.

Notes:

Juniperus sabina
Savin

Description: There are about 50 Species in this Genus, only three of which are terribly toxic: *J. sabina*, native to southern and central Europe; and *J. horizontalis* and *J. virginiana*, native to North America. They are all evergreen shrubs or trees growing to 12 feet tall by 12 feet wide. The leaves, like most members of the Cypress family, are scale-like and blue-green in color. The flowers are almost unnoticeable, leading to berry-like cones that are at first blue, and turn white. All parts of the plant smell terrible when crushed.

Cultivation: Savins (and most other Cedars) are hardy in all but the harshest of climates. The seeds, due to their hard outer coat, require a period of cold stratification prior to planting. Soaking the seed in boiling water for a few seconds may help speed the germination process. Plant well-established seedlings in a sunny location in the spring. Propagation may also be achieved by wood cuttings.

Parts Used: All parts.

Poison: All parts, especially the young twigs. Toxicity Level I.

Side Effects: Within just an hour or so of ingestion, nausea, vomiting, cardiac arrhythmia, tachycardia and convulsions have been reported, followed by severe internal bleeding, uterine contractions, kidney and liver damage and respiratory arrest. Death occurs anywhere from a half day to several days afterward by respiratory paralysis and arrest. The oil can cause blistering and necrotic scars if it comes into contact with skin.

Medicinal Uses: Savin has a long history of use as an abortifacient and insecticide. Topically, the oil was used to treat warts. The plants in North America are also used as an abortifacient and insecticide. Reports of bathing rheumatic body parts in a steam of the boughs have also been recorded, as well as an infusion of the leaves and fruits taken to treat coughs.

Magical Uses: All three plants have been used as incense in shamanic undertakings and Native American ceremonies and purification rites. Placing the boughs on a tepee pole is said to ward off lightning. (For those of us who do not live in tepees, I suggest attaching them to a chimney.)

Interesting Tidbits: The bark yields a mahogany-colored dye.

The Cheyenne burn the leaves as incense in ceremonies to remove a fear of thunder; several other tribes use the plant in funeral rites.

Notes:

Kalmia spp.
Mountain Laurel, Calico Bush, Sheep Laurel

Description: A Genus of about eight Species, Kalmia are evergreen shrubs, growing in moist places in eastern North America; one is native to Cuba. Resembling Rhododendrons (and often mistaken for them) they can grow up to thirty-five feet high with rough, branched stems having small, simple, leathery green leaves. The flowers are white, pink or purple in corymbs (groups) of ten to fifty, and appear in mid-summer. The fruit are small capsules, almost the same color as the bark.

Cultivation: Difficult to cultivate either by seed or cuttings, Kalmia are now mostly propagated by tissue culture, something best done by horticulturalists. Plant your purchased seedling or small shrub in a cool, moist, acidic soil in partial shade to full sun. Kalmia grow best when they are in a protected setting. While they may be sold as "shade tolerant", they will not bloom or only sparsely bloom if not exposed to sun.

Parts Used: Twigs, leaves.

Poison: The leaves and nectar. Toxicity Level I.

Side Effects: Ingestion causes nausea, vomiting, burning in the mouth and throat, diarrhea, hypotension, and progressive paralysis leading to death. Similar to Rhododendron, the honey produced by bees feeding on Kalmia is also toxic.

Medicinal Uses: Leaf infusions, twig decoctions and powdered leaves are used variously to treat head colds, headaches, to ease the pain of neuralgia and for bowel complaints. A leaf poultice is used for swellings and sprains. A leaf wash is used as an insect repellant, an ointment as a liniment for sore muscles.

Magical Uses: None known.

Interesting Tidbits: The plant's toxicity has been known by Native Americans for centuries – a decoction of the leaves was drunk to commit suicide.

The leaves of *K. latifolia* are used by the Mahuna tribe as a deodorant. The wood is used by the Cherokee to carve decorations.

Notes:

Larrea tridentata
Chaparral, Creosote Bush

Description: The *Larrea* Genus is comprised of five Species, all native to south and western North America. *L. tridentata* is an evergreen bush, growing about 10 feet tall. The leaves are dark green and resinous. Flowers have five petals, are yellow and about an inch in diameter. The entire plant gives off a smell similar to creosote, hence the common name.

Cultivation: *Larrea* are happiest in a desert-like situation and more easily propagated by root division and transplanting. Seeds should be leached by submersing them in running water for about twelve hours, then planting indoors in a rich soil and allowed to harden-off before being moved outside to their permanent location. Young plants will die off quickly in drought conditions but older plants aren't as susceptible to that sort of stress.

Parts Used: Twigs, leaves.

Poison: The aerial parts of the plant. Toxicity Level II.

Side Effects: Dermatitis may be experienced by some when contacting any part of the plant. Ingestion may cause nausea, vomiting, diarrhea, and abdominal cramps; renal and liver damage have been reported. Death is rare but not unknown.

Medicinal Uses: An infusion of the twigs and/or leaves is used in the treatment of tuberculosis and other chest complaints, as a cold remedy and to relieve menstrual cramps. Externally, an infusion of the leaves is used as a wash to treat chickenpox, ease rheumatic pains. The leaves are used as a poultice for sores, wounds, insect bites and applied to the penis to treat gonorrhea.

Magical Uses: None known.

Interesting Tidbits: The "King Clone" is a single colony cluster of Creosote Bushes in the Central Mojave Desert near Lucerne Valley, California. It is estimated to be 11,700 years old, making it one of the oldest living organisms on Earth.

In the *Dune* series by Frank Herbert, the Fremen rub the juice of the creosote bush into their hands to prevent water loss through the skin not covered by their suits.

The plant is host to an insect that produces lac and deposits it on the stems. The lac is malleable when heated but hardens again when cooled, making it a perfect sealing wax. This lac is also used to make awl handles.

The charcoaled wood is used in tattooing as a greenish-blue color.

Notes:

Melia azedarach
Chinaberry, Persian Lilac

Description: Five Species are native to Asia and Australia but Chinaberry trees can be found as ornamentals throughout the world. It is deciduous or semi-evergreen, growing up to fifty feet tall. The twigs have a purplish bark which matures to a reddish gray. The leaves are long, pinnate and glossy green. Lilac-colored, sweetly smelling flowers appear in spring, giving way to smooth green berries that become yellowish and wrinkled at maturity.

Cultivation: Prefers a warmish climate, similar to the southern United States. Seeds may be planted before last frost, or cold stratify them for a couple of weeks before planting. Chinaberry can also be successfully started from cuttings or dividing suckers off the main root stock. They will easily self-pollinate and are considered invasive plants in many parts of the United States.

Parts Used: Leaves, Bark, Berries.

Poison: All, but especially the fruit and bark. Toxicity Level: I-II.

Side Effects: Nausea, vomiting, diarrhea, cold sweats, respiratory distress, muscular spasms, convulsions. Fatalities are rare but have occurred. The toxicity level appears to vary from plant to plant.

Medicinal Uses: The Cherokee use an infusion of the bark and root internally for worms and as a fomentation externally to treat ringworm.

An infusion of the leaves was used in the past to induce uterine relaxation.

Magical Uses: The fruit are used as beads in good luck charms.

Interesting Tidbits: The Chinaberry tree is related to Mahogany and as such, its wood is used in similar situations. Due to its color, it's often mistaken for Burmese Teak.

Some birds, such as hummingbirds, have been known to gorge on the fruit and fly around in a drunken state.

The leaves, when crushed, become a potent insecticide.

Notes:

Nerium oleander
Oleander

Description: *Nerium* is a monotype Genus. In other words, it has only one Species. While you may think there are many Species due to the variety of flower colors, they are simply cultivars. Oleander is an evergreen shrub thought to be native to the Mediterranean. It grows up to twenty feet tall but is usually trimmed to no more than ten feet due to the fact that it can easily become leggy. The dark green, oblong, leathery leaves are distinctive with a white stripe down the middle. The flowers appear in clusters and can be almost any color but generally white, pink or red. Seed pods are long and narrow like the leaves and when mature, they split open to reveal downy seeds resembling colored milkweed seeds.

Cultivation: Naturalized in many parts of the world, Oleander is a popular garden or hedge shrub. Hardy in USDA zones 8-10, it prefers full sun and although it will survive dry conditions, prefers moisture and humidity. Propagation is easiest by cuttings rooted in summer. Propagation by seed is also possible.

Parts Used: Leaves.

Poison: All parts of the plant. Toxicity Level I.

Side Effects: Sensitive individuals may experience contact dermatitis when touching any part of the plant. Symptoms present themselves quickly. Ingestion leads to numbness of the tongue and throat, followed by severe nausea, vomiting, and muscular spasms. Slowing of the heartbeat and/or arrhythmia precedes coma and finally death approximately five hours later.

Medicinal Uses: The use of Oleander has been documented for more than 1,500 years for a wide variety of skin conditions as well as asthma, epilepsy, malaria and as a heart tonic.

Theophrastus said that the root of Oleander administered in wine "makes the temper gentler and more cheerful".

As with all extremely toxic herbs, it has been used both as an abortifacient and for suicide.

An extract has been used in China to treat congestive heart failure and in the control of atrial fibrillation. It is currently being investigated as an anti-cancer agent.

Magical Uses: Traditionally used in spells for attracting love.

Interesting Tidbits: Oleander is the official flower of the city of Hiroshima, Japan. It was the first to flower after the atomic bombing in 1945.

One Greek legend holds that the plant got its name and magical correspondence (love and romance) from Hero, a priestess of Aphrodite. Her lover, Leander, would swim the Hellespont to see her every night. One night he was drowned in a tempest. When Hero saw his body dashed against the rocks, she cried, "Oh, Leander. Oh, Leander." In his hand was clutched an Oleander flower. She subsequently couldn't live without him and committed suicide.

The pirate, Jean Lafitte, also figures into the Oleander naming legend. It is said he attacked a Norwegian schooner and killed all the passengers, except for one man clinging to a flowering bush. That man's name was Ole Anderson. Lafitte hired him as his personal gardener at his compound on Galveston Island, calling the man "Olea Ander". Lafitte later named the plant after the man.

An urban legend circulates about a Boy Scout troop that died after roasting hot dogs on Oleander sticks. A similar story is found in an 1844 publication, referencing an 1809 incident in France. A scientific study in 2005 found negligible amounts of toxins in the hot dogs, while also finding that both fresh and dried oleander sticks presented mechanical difficulties making their use as roasting skewers impractical.

In India, Hindu mourners place the flower around the bodies of dead relatives.

Notes:

Physostigma venenosum
Calabar Bean, Ordeal Bean

Description: A native to West Africa, this Genus has four Species. It is a strong perennial creeper or climber, growing up to fifty feet in length with large leaves and pale pink or purple flowers. The seed pod may be up to seven inches long and generally contains two or three dark brown seeds. The seeds ripen year round but are most abundant during the rainy season (June to September in its native habitat).

Cultivation: Requires a subtropical or tropical climate, well-drained, rich soil and a moderate amount of water and humidity.

Parts Used: Seed.

Poison: The seed. Toxicity Level I.

Side Effects: Ingestion disrupts the communication between the nerves and muscles. Initial sensation is numbness in arms and legs, followed by the appearance of severe intoxication. Death occurs quickly from respiratory and cardiac arrest.

Medicinal Uses: The chief chemical constituent, physostigmine (now synthesized), has been used in the treatment of glaucoma since the 1920's and more recently to relieve the symptoms of myasthenia gravis. At one time, a preparation of Calabar was used in the treatment of chronic constipation, and to relax muscular spasms associated with epilepsy and acute tetanus.

Magical Uses: None known.

Interesting Tidbits: According to a report from the missionary W. Daniell in 1840, the Efik people used the bean in trials by ordeal, especially in trials of witchcraft. As in all similar trials, if the accused lived, innocence was declared. The bean can be swallowed whole with little effect but some duels were decided by two men each eating one half of a bean.

Notes:

Rhus toxicodendron
Poison Ivy

Description: There are approximately 200 Species in the *Rhus* Genus, only some of which are toxic. Poison Ivy is generally a climber but may be found as a shrub or even a small tree. It's native to North and Central America but has traveled the world. Its most distinguishing characteristic is the large, trifoliate leaves (they grow in threes on the stalk). Greenish-white flowers appear in June, followed by clusters of berry-like fruit.

Cultivation: Grows wild almost anywhere and why would you want to cultivate it? However, it prefers moist soil and partial shade.

Parts Used: Leaves, essential oil.

Poison: All parts of the plant. Toxicity Level I.

Side Effects: *Most* people experience severe contact dermatitis when coming into contact with the plant.

Urushiol, the offending oil, will stay on clothing until washed and therefore, you may erupt in a rash from touching contaminated clothes. The dermatitis can last for weeks. Getting the oil into the eye can cause blindness. Ingestion causes severe irritation of the mouth, throat and gastrointestinal tract, followed by nausea, vomiting, bloody diarrhea, dizziness, heart palpitations and may cause serious kidney damage.

Medicinal Uses: No longer in use but was once used to counteract rashes associated with Nettle sting and other skin eruptions. It is still used homeopathically to treat rheumatism, ringworm and other skin diseases.

Magical Uses: None known.

Interesting Tidbits: The juice is used as an indelible ink for marking linen, as well as an ingredient in some boot polishes and lacquers.

Notes:

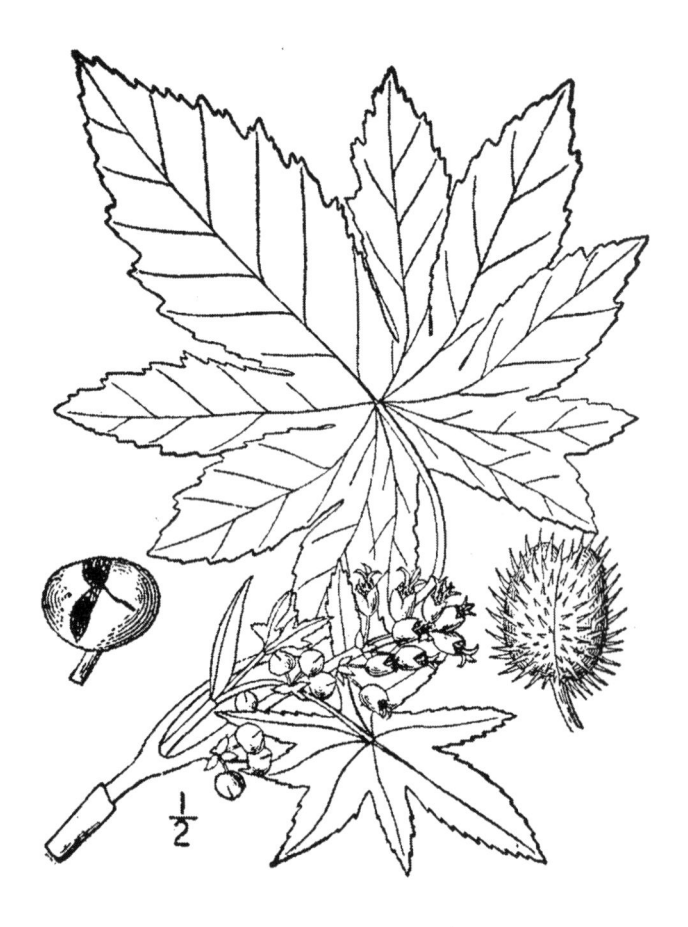

Ricinus communis

Ricinus communis
Castor, Palma Christi

Description: Another monotype Genus, Castor is a sizeable shrub with large, hand-shaped leaves growing from purplish stalks. The leaves are red and shiny when young, turning a blue-green color as they mature. The plant produces both male and female flowers on the same plant. These are a light green color, the females having a reddish calyx. The fruit is a spiny capsule containing three seeds.

Cultivation: Soak the seeds in warm water for a day then sow them outdoors after the danger of frost has passed. It prefers rich, well-drained soil and full sun. Depending on growing conditions, it may need staking to stay upright. Considered a perennial in USDA zones 8 and above, however, it will readily self-sow after the first year and is considered invasive in some parts.

Parts Used: Seed.

Poison: The seed. Toxicity Level I.

Side Effects: Symptoms appear several hours after ingestion and may include nausea, bloody diarrhea, vomiting, intestinal inflammation, liver and kidney damage. Death occurs from circulatory failure.

Medicinal Uses: An oil pressed from the seed (and then heated to remove the toxins) is an ages-old remedy for constipation and has been known since at least 4000 BCE as a purgative.

Warm Castor Oil packs are used for sore muscles. It was also dropped into the eye to ease irritation after removal of a foreign body. Externally, the oil is used to ease the itch of various skin complaints.

The Degueño mash the bean and add it to an ointment for acne. Navajo women use the plant to become sterile. The fresh leaves are used as a poultice by nursing mothers of the Canary Islands to increase the flow of milk.

Magical Uses: A bean carried on one's person will confer protection. In the tradition of Apuleius, it will ward off hail and storms from a traveler.

Interesting Tidbits: Stories abound, even today, of poisoning by Ricin, which is simply a powdered bean. In 1978, Bulgarian dissident Georgi Markov was killed by a Ricin pellet fired into him by a modified umbrella.

Allegedly, Cleopatra applied the oil to the whites of her eyes to brighten them.

Also allegedly, Mussolini's henchmen would force political opponents to drink castor oil to "cure their opposition", sometimes up to a liter. While not fatal, it would certainly be unpleasant.

Castor Oil was also used in the manufacture of artificial leather and rubber, as well as in furniture polish. At one time, it was an ingredient in the manufacture of fly paper. Today, it is used for biodiesel.

This Castor Oil is not to be confused with "Oil of Castor" or "Castoreum", which comes from glands near the anus of beavers.

Notes:

Strychnos nux-vomica
Nux Vomica, Quaker Buttons

Description: There are approximately 190 Species in this Genus, not all of which are toxic. This particular plant is an evergreen tree (up to 75 feet), native to India and the Malay Peninsula. It has spiny branches and shiny leaves, characterized by three veins. The flowers are greenish-white, giving way to an orange or yellow fruit about the size of an apple. The seeds, usually 5-8 in each fruit, are disc-shaped and densely covered with satiny hairs.

Cultivation: Requires a subtropical or tropical climate. Seeds should be soaked in warm water for a day then sown in a rich, loamy soil in shady conditions. Seedlings should be transplanted to at least 20 feet apart when mature. Flowering happens approximately three years after planting.

Parts Used: Seeds.

Poison: The seed. Toxicity Level I.

Side Effects: The chief chemical constituent is Strychnine, which causes strong convulsions. Death is by asphyxia or cardiac arrest and can occur within a few minutes or a few hours. This plant is not as forgiving as the Calabar.

Medicinal Uses: Once employed as a stimulant and tonic, mostly in the cases of chronic constipation. It was also used in analgesic ointments. One preparation was sold as a "nerve tonic" in Europe as late as the 1970's.

The fruit is used in India in the treatment of blood disorders, hemorrhoids, jaundice and ulcers.

Magical Uses: None known.

Interesting Tidbits: The toxicity of strychnine has been known for centuries, recommended by Porta to kill dogs. The seed was and is used as a rat poison.

Deaths have been reported of Strychnine poisoning occurring from snorting adulterated cocaine.

One of the treatments of Strychnine poisoning is the administration of curare, a poison from a South American relative, *S. toxifera.*

Notes:

Taxus baccata
Yew

Description: Seven Species comprise this Genus, only one of which is native to North America. The common Yew is native to most of Europe and Asia Minor. It is a tree growing 40 to 50 feet high with reddish brown, peeling bark and dark green leaves or needles. Each tree is unisexual. The cone, or fruit, resembles a red (sometimes yellow) olive and encloses a single seed. The seed covering, or aril, is the only part of the tree that isn't toxic.

Cultivation: Seeds should be sown as soon as they are ripe, either in a cold frame or in containers. Germination may take two or more years. Semi-ripe cuttings taken in late summer or early fall should overwinter in a cold frame. Yew tolerates most soil conditions but will not be happy if waterlogged. It grows best if started in rich soil in sun to partial shade. Once established, it will tolerate shady conditions. A well-cared-for tree or hedge will grow about a foot a year but these trees are long-lived: the Fortingall Yew in Perthshire, Scotland is thought to be 2,000 to 5,000 years old. It's impossible to determine the exact age of a Yew. Ring-dating is unreliable as parts of the tree die off while new trunks arise from the same root and branches may become hollow with age.

Parts Used: Leaves.

Poison: All parts of the plant except the seed aril. Toxicity Level I.

Side Effects: Within an hour of ingestion, nausea, vomiting, dizziness, and diarrhea are experienced, followed by kidney damage. Severe toxicity includes excited then depressed respiration, followed by respiratory and circulatory failure, coma then death usually within 24 hours.

Medicinal Uses: *Always* known as a poison, yet in 1021 Avicenna introduced a cardiac drug made from *T. baccata*. Today, the chemotherapy drug Paclitaxel is derived from the English Yew as it is considered a more renewable resource than *T. brevifolia*, which yielded the drug Taxol.

The plant is used to treat breast and ovarian cancer in the Central Himalayas.

Magical Uses: Has been used in rituals to raise the dead, for cursing and protection yet is generally avoided due to the known toxicity.

In Devonshire, to ensure fertility, a male should walk backward around a tree; if female, you should walk forward.

Yew branches are used in Ireland on Palm Sunday. After the service, the branches are placed in the house and byres for good luck, then burned to make the ash for Ash Wednesday celebrations.

Interesting Tidbits: As stated earlier, the toxicity of Yew has long been known. Nicander (200 BCE) describes the painful death; the Celtic chieftain Catuvolcus (53 BCE) preferred death by Yew rather than becoming a Roman slave.

Porta describes spies using powdered Yew to ulcerate their skin and make them unrecognizable. (The remedy is the juice of Poplar.)

Shakespeare described the contents of Hekate's cauldron as "slips of yew, silver'd in the moon's eclipse" (Macbeth).

Yew has long been known as the source of the English longbows, the oldest of which is said to be radiocarbon dated between 4040 BCE and 3640 BCE. It can be seen at The National Museum of Scotland. Indeed, in Shakespeare's *Richard III*, Scroop says, "Thy very beadsmen/Learn to bend their bows/Of double-fatal Yew/Against thy state".

The Yew was a prized wood for the construction of lutes in the Medieval, Renaissance and Baroque eras.

Amongst many literary references, in the *Harry Potter* series, Voldemort carries a wand made of Yew.

Notes:

Cheat Sheet

Common	Latin
Aconite	*Aconitum spp.*
Adam and Eve	*Arum maculatum*
Agave	*Agave tequilana*
Alkanet	*Alkanna tinctoria*
Alkanna	*Alkanna tinctoria*
Aloe	*Aloe ferox*
Angel's Trumpet	*Brugmansia suaveolens*
Apple	*Malus domestica*
Arbor-Vitae	*Thuja occidentalis*
Arnica	*Arnica montana*
Autumn Crocus	*Colchicum autumnale*
Azalea	*Rhododendron spp.*
Balsam Pear	*Momordica charantia*
Barberry	*Berberis vulgaris*
Belladonna	*Atropa belladonna*
Betel Nut	*Areca catechu*
Bitter Orange	*Citrus aurantium*
Bloodroot	*Sanguinaria canadensis*
Blue Cohosh	*Caulophyllum thalactroides*
Borage	*Borago officinalis*

Box	*Buxus sempervirens*
Broom	*Cytisus scoparius*
Bryony, White	*Bryonia dioica*
Buckthorn	*Rhamnus cathartica*
Calabar Bean	*Physostigma venenosum*
Camphor	*Cinnamomum camphora*
Carolina Jessamine	*Gelsemium spp.*
Castor Bean	*Ricinus communis*
Celandine	*Chelidonium majus*
Chaparral	*Larrea tridentata*
Cherry Laurel	*Prunus laurocerasus*
Chinaberry	*Melia azerdarach*
Club Moss	*Lycopodium clavatum*
Columbine	*Aquilegia vulgaris*
Cotton	*Gossypium spp.*
Cyclamen	*Cyclamen persicum*
Daffodil	*Narcissum spp.*
Damiana	*Turnera diffusa*
Daphne	*Daphne spp.*
Datura	*Datura stramonium*
Deadly Nightshade	*Atropa belladonna*
Dieffenbachia	*Dieffenbachia seguine*
Dittany	*Dictamnus albus*

Dyer's Bugloss	*Alkanna tinctoria*
Euonymus	*Euonymus europaeus*
Fly Agaric	*Amanita muscaria*
Foxglove	*Digitalis purpurea*
Fumitory	*Fumaria officinalis*
Gelsemium	*Gelsemium spp.*
Golden Chain	*Laburnum anagyroides*
Goldenseal	*Hydrastis canadensis*
Gymnema	*Gymnema sylvestre*
Hellebore	*Helleborus spp.*
Hemlock	*Conium maculatum*
Hemp	*Cannabis sativa*
Henbane	*Hyoscyamus niger*
Holly	*Ilex aquifolium*
Horse Chestnut	*Aesculus hippocastanum*
Indigo	*Baptisia australis*
Ivy, Common	*Hedera helix*
Jessamine, Yellow	*Gelsemium spp.*
Jimson Weed	*Datura stramonium*
Jojoba	*Simmondsia chinensis*
Kalanchoe	*Kalanchoe lanceolata*
Kola Nut	*Cola spp.*
Laburnum	*Laburnum anagyroides*

Larkspur	*Delphinium spp.*
Lily of the Valley	*Convallaria majalis*
Lima Bean	*Phaseolus lunatus*
Lobelia	*Lobelia inflata*
Mace	*Myristica fragrans*
Mandrake	*Mandragora officinarum*
Marijuana	*Cannabis sativa*
May Apple	*Podophyllum peltatum*
Meadow Saffron	*Colchicum autumnale*
Milkweed	*Asclepias tuberosa*
Mistletoe	*Viscum album*
Monkshood	*Aconitum spp.*
Morning Glory	*Convolvulus spp.*
Mountain Laurel	*Kalmia latifolia*
Mustard, Black	*Brassica nigra*
Narcissus	*Narcissum spp.*
Nutmeg	*Myristica fragrans*
Nux Vomica	*Strychnos nux-vomica*
Oleander	*Nerium oleander*
Opium Poppy	*Papaver somniferum*
Pasque Flower	*Pulsatilla vulgaris*
Pennyroyal	*Mentha pulegium*
Persian Lilac	*Melia azedarach*

Poison Ivy	*Rhus toxicodendron*
Poke	*Phytolacca*
Poppy, White	*Papaver somniferum*
Potato	*Solanum tuberosum*
Quaker's Buttons	*Strychnos nux-vomica*
Rhododendron	*Rhododendron spp*
Rhubarb	*Rheum raponticum*
Rosary Pea	*Abrus precatorius*
Rue	*Ruta graveolens*
Saffron	*Crocus sativus*
Sassafras	*Sassafras officinale*
Savin	*Juniperus sabina*
Scarlet Pimpernel	*Anagallis arvensis*
Suicide Tree	*Cerbera odollam*
Sweet Flag	*Acorus calamus*
Tansy	*Chrysanthemum vulgare*
Thornapple	*Datura stramonium*
Water Hemlock	*Cicuta virosa*
Wild Lettuce	*Lactuca virosa*
Wintergreen	*Gaultheria procumbens*
Wormwood	*Artemisia absinthium*
Yew	*Taxus baccata*
Yohimbe	*Pausinystalia yohimbe*

SELECTED BIBLIOGRAPHY

Bergen, Fanny D. (editor). *Animal and Plant Lore*. New York, NY: Houghton, Mifflin & Co., 1899

Bevan-Jones, Robert *Poisonous Plants: A Cultural and Social History*. Oxford, UK: Windgather Press, 2009

Culpeper, Nicholas. *Culpeper's Complete Herbal*. London, UK: W. Foulsham & Co., Ltd., no date.

de Cleene, Marcel & Marie Claire Lejeune. *Compendium of Symbolic and Ritual Plants of Europe*. Ghent, Belgium: Man & Culture Publishers, 2003

Dillaire, Claudia R. *Egyptian Revenge Spells*. Berkeley, CA: Crossing Press, 2009

Ellacombe, Rev. Henry N. *The Plant-Lore and Garden-Craft of Shakespeare*. London, UK: W. Satchell & Co., 1884 (Project Gutenberg eBook 2009)

Ellis, David. *Medicinal Herbs and Poisonous Plants.* LaVergne, TN: Davidson Press, 2008 (reprint of a 1918 book)

Gerard, John (updated by Robert Thompson). *The Herball or Generall Historie of Plantes.* London, UK: Norton & Whitaker, 1633

Gomez, Julie. *A Guide to Deadly Herbs.* Blaine, WA: Hancock House Publishers, 1997

Gottlieb, Adam. *Legal Highs: A Concise Encyclopedia of Legal Herbs and Chemicals with Psychoactive Properties.* Manhattan Beach, CA: 20th Century Alchemist, 1973

Gow, A.S.F. & A. F. Scholfield, editors. *Poems and Poetical Fragments; Nicander of Colophon* New York, NY: Cambridge University Press, 1953

Grieve, M. *A Modern Herbal.* Mineola, NY: Dover Publications, 1971

Kautilya. *The Arthashastra* New Delhi, India: Penguin Books, 1992

Leyel, Mrs. C. F. *Magic of Herbs* London, UK: Butler & Tanner, Ltd., 1926 (reprinted 2009, Health Research Books, Pomeroy, WA)

MacInnis, Peter. *Poisons: From Hemlock to Botox and the Killer Bean Calabar.* New York, NY: Arcade Publishing, 2011

Martin, Deborah J. *Herbs: Medicinal, Magical, Marvelous!* Winchester, UK: O-Books, 2009

Mayor, Adrienne. *Greek Fire, Poison Arrows, and Scorpion Bombs.* Woodstock, NY: The Overlook Press, 2009

Mead, Richard. *A Mechanical Account of Poisons in Several Essays, 4th ed.* London, UK: J. Brindley, Bookseller, 1747

Miller, Richard Alan. *The Magical and Ritual Use of Herbs.* Rochester, VT: Destiny Books, 1983

Moerman, Daniel E. *Native American Ethnobotany*. London, UK: Timber Press, 1998

Porta, John Baptista. *Natural Magick in 20 Books*. London, UK: Thomas Young & Samuel Speed, 1658

Schultes, Richard Evans & Albert Hofmann. *Plants of the Gods*. Rochester, VT: Healing Arts Press, 1992

Stevens, Serita Deborah & Anne Klarner. *Deadly Doses: A Writer's Guide to Poisons*. Cincinnati, OH: Writer's Digest Books, 1990

Stewart, Amy. *Wicked Plants*. Chapel Hill, NC: Algonquin Books of Chapel Hill, 2009

Theophrastus (translated by Sir Arthur Hoart). *Enquiry into Plants and Minor Works on Odours & Weather Signs)* c. 300 BC (read on Google Books)

Thompson, C. J. S. *Poison Mysteries in History, Romance and Crime*. London, UK: The Scientific Press Ltd., 1923

Vickery, Roy. *Oxford Dictionary of Plant Lore*. Oxford, UK: Oxford University Press, 1995

Wink, Michael & Ben-Erik van Wyk. *Mind-Altering and Poisonous Plants of the World*. London, UK: Timber Press, 2008

ILLUSTRATIONS

Aesculus hippocastanum: USDA-NRCS PLANTS Database / Britton, N.L., and A. Brown. 1913. An illustrated flora of the northern United States, Canada and the British Possessions. 3 vols. Charles Scribner's Sons, New York. Vol. 2: 498.

Aquilegia vulgaris: USDA-NRCS PLANTS Database / Britton, N.L., and A. Brown. 1913. An illustrated flora of the northern United States, Canada and the British Possessions. 3 vols. Charles Scribner's Sons, New York. Vol. 2: 93.

Artemisia absinthium: USDA-NRCS PLANTS Database / Britton, N.L., and A. Brown. 1913. An illustrated flora of the northern United States, Canada and the British Possessions. 3 vols. Charles Scribner's Sons, New York. Vol. 3: 525.

Brassica Nigra: USDA-NRCS PLANTS Database / Britton, N.L., and A. Brown. 1913. An illustrated flora of the northern United States, Canada and the British Possessions. 3 vols. Charles Scribner's Sons, New York. Vol. 2: 193.

Cannabis sativa: USDA-NRCS PLANTS Database / Britton, N.L., and A. Brown. 1913. An illustrated flora of the northern United States, Canada and the British Possessions. 3 vols. Charles Scribner's Sons, New York. Vol. 1: 634.

Chelidonium majus: USDA-NRCS PLANTS Database / Britton, N.L., and A. Brown. 1913. An illustrated flora of the northern United States, Canada and the British Possessions. 3 vols. Charles Scribner's Sons, New York. Vol. 2: 141

Cicuta maculata: USDA-NRCS PLANTS Database / USDA NRCS. Wetland flora: Field office illustrated guide to plant species. USDA Natural Resources Conservation Service.

Colchicum autumnale: L. H. Bailey Standard Cyclopedia of Horticulture (New York, New York: The MacMillan Company, 1917). Retrieved May 1, 2013 from http://etc.usf.edu/clipart/84100/84139/84139_colchicum_au.htm

Conium maculatum: USDA-NRCS PLANTS Database / Britton, N.L., and A. Brown. 1913. An illustrated flora of the northern United States, Canada and the British Possessions. 3 vols. Charles Scribner's Sons, New York. Vol. 2: 653.

Convallaria majalis: USDA-NRCS PLANTS Database / Britton, N.L., and A. Brown. 1913. An illustrated flora of the northern United States, Canada and the British Possessions. 3 vols. Charles Scribner's Sons, New York. Vol. 1: 522.

Crocus sativus: L. H. Bailey Standard Cyclopedia of Horticulture (New York, New York: The MacMillan Company, 1917). Retrieved May 1, 2013 from http://etc.usf.edu/clipart/84200/84261/84261_crocus_sativ.htm

Cytisus scoparius: USDA-NRCS PLANTS Database / Britton, N.L., and A. Brown. 1913. An illustrated flora of the northern United States, Canada and the British Possessions. 3 vols. Charles Scribner's Sons, New York. Vol. 2: 350

Daphne mezereum: USDA-NRCS PLANTS Database / Britton, N.L., and A. Brown. 1913. An illustrated flora of the northern United States, Canada and the British Possessions. 3 vols. Charles Scribner's Sons, New York. Vol. 2: 574

Datura stramonium: USDA-NRCS PLANTS Database / Britton, N.L., and A. Brown. 1913. An illustrated flora of the northern United States, Canada and the British Possessions. 3 vols. Charles Scribner's Sons, New York. Vol. 3: 169.

Delphinium tricorne: USDA-NRCS PLANTS Database / Britton, N.L., and A. Brown. 1913. An illustrated flora of the northern United States, Canada and the British Possessions. 3 vols. Charles Scribner's Sons, New York. Vol. 2: 96.

Digitalis purpurea: USDA-NRCS PLANTS Database / Britton, N.L., and A. Brown. 1913. An illustrated flora of the northern United States, Canada and the British Possessions. 3 vols. Charles Scribner's Sons, New York. Vol. 3: 204.

Gaultheria procumbens: USDA-NRCS PLANTS Database / USDA NRCS. Wetland flora: Field office illustrated guide to plant species. USDA Natural Resources Conservation Service.

Gelsemium sempervirens: USDA-NRCS PLANTS Database / USDA NRCS. Wetland flora: Field office illustrated guide to plant species. USDA Natural Resources Conservation Service.

Helleborus viridis: USDA-NRCS PLANTS Database / Britton, N.L., and A. Brown. 1913. An illustrated flora of the northern United States, Canada and the British Possessions. 3 vols. Charles Scribner's Sons, New York. Vol. 2: 87.

Hyoscyamus niger: USDA-NRCS PLANTS Database / Britton, N.L., and A. Brown. 1913. An illustrated flora of the northern United States, Canada and the British Possessions. 3 vols. Charles Scribner's Sons, New York. Vol. 3: 169.

Ipomoea pandurata: USDA-NRCS PLANTS Database / Britton, N.L., and A. Brown. 1913. An illustrated flora of the northern United States, Canada and the British Possessions. 3 vols. Charles Scribner's Sons, New York. Vol. 3: 43.

Lactuca virosa: USDA-NRCS PLANTS Database / Britton, N.L., and A. Brown. 1913. An illustrated flora of the northern United States, Canada and the British Possessions. 3 vols. Charles Scribner's Sons, New York. Vol. 3: 318.

Lobelia inflata: USDA-NRCS PLANTS Database / Britton, N.L., and A. Brown. 1913. An illustrated flora of the northern United States, Canada and the British Possessions. 3 vols. Charles Scribner's Sons, New York. Vol. 3: 303.

Lycopodium clavatum: USDA-NRCS PLANTS Database / Britton, N.L., and A. Brown. 1913. An illustrated flora of the northern United States, Canada and the British Possessions. 3 vols. Charles Scribner's Sons, New York. Vol. 1: 47.

Papaver somniferum: USDA-NRCS PLANTS Database / Britton, N.L., and A. Brown. 1913. An illustrated flora of the northern United States, Canada and the British Possessions. 3 vols. Charles Scribner's Sons, New York. Vol. 2: 137.

Podophyllum peltatum: USDA-NRCS PLANTS Database / Britton, N.L., and A. Brown. 1913. An illustrated flora of the northern United States, Canada and the British Possessions. 3 vols. Charles Scribner's Sons, New York. Vol. 2: 130.

Phytolacca americana: USDA-NRCS PLANTS Database / USDA NRCS. Wetland flora: Field office illustrated guide to plant species. USDA Natural Resources Conservation Service.

Rhododendron canescens: USDA-NRCS PLANTS Database / Britton, N.L., and A. Brown. 1913. An illustrated flora of the northern United States, Canada and the British Possessions. 3 vols. Charles Scribner's Sons, New York. Vol. 2: 678.

Ricinus communis: USDA-NRCS PLANTS Database / Britton, N.L., and A. Brown. 1913. An illustrated flora of the northern United States, Canada and the British Possessions. 3 vols. Charles Scribner's Sons, New York. Vol. 2: 461.

Sanguinaria Canadensis: USDA-NRCS PLANTS Database / Britton, N.L., and A. Brown. 1913. An illustrated flora of the northern United States, Canada and the British Possessions. 3 vols. Charles Scribner's Sons, New York. Vol. 2: 140.

ABOUT THE AUTHOR

Deborah J. "DJ" Martin left the frozen tundra (Minnesota) many moons ago and now lives in the north Georgia mountains with her husband, their crazy cats and numerous woodland creatures. She is the author of *Herbs: Medicinal, Magical, Marvelous!* (O-Books, 2009) and *A Green Witch's Formulary* (Balboa Press, 2011), as well as the urban fantasy novel *Stressed! Ogre's Assistant Book One* (available in e-book format on Amazon and Smashwords).

If she's not clickety-punching numbers for her accounting clients or writing, you can probably find her in the garden, visiting her grandchildren or in her recliner with her nose stuck in a book.

Made in the USA
Lexington, KY
28 June 2013